The materiality of reading

The materiality of reading

Edited by Theresa Schilhab & Sue Walker

Aarhus University Press

The matcriality of reading

Cover, layout and typesetting: Paul Luna
Publishing editor: Jakob Jørgensen Vestergaard
This book is typeset in Eskorte Latin and Mundo Sans
and printed on 130g Munken Lynx
Printed by Narayana Press, Denmark

Printed in Denmark 2020
1st edition, 1st impression

ISBN 978 87 7184 958 5

Aarhus University Press
aarhusuniversitypress.dk

International distributors
Oxbow Books Ltd., oxbowbooks.com
ISD, isdistribution.com

The cover illustration is based on the Oxford University Press typesetting of the Mouse's Tale, which was approved by Lewis Carroll in 1880.

PEER
REVIEWED

/ In accordance with requirements of the Danish Ministry of Higher Education and Science, the certification means that a PhD level peer has made a written assessment justifying this book's scientific quality.

FSC
www.fsc.org
MIX
Paper from responsible sources
FSC® C010651

Contents

Engaging with the text

Introduction

Theresa Schilhab & Sue Walker

The phrase 'materiality of reading' may be interpreted in different ways, since there are numerous disciplinary perspectives on what constitutes materiality. This collection of essays is a result of discussions between members of the European research initiative E-READ ("Evolution of Reading in the Age of Digitisation" (2014–2019), funded by European Cooperation in Science & Technology (COST)), which brought together nearly 200 scholars and scientists studying numerous aspects of reading. Our anthology addresses the materiality of reading from novel perspectives influenced to some extent by the editors' academic backgrounds in neurobiology and embodied reading, and typography and design for reading. We asked for ideas and work in progress (rather than final research studies) about materiality, so that we could capture some of the debate that occurred in the E-READ meetings – in Zadar, Vilnius, Reading and Stavanger.

The materiality of reading is about the interaction between a person and an object where the person uses different senses to know and understand the object and the object is a more or less considered manifestation of a content. This materiality can also involve the comfort experienced while reading, the space (where we read) and the act of reading (how we read). Materiality also plays a pivotal role in who is included or excluded as a reader. It influences our access to texts, as well as the ease of reading and kinds of user engagement that are possible. For typographers and book designers, the materiality of reading is about making text and pictures accessible, legible, intriguing and enjoyable, recognising that different kinds of readers and circumstances of use should impact on the visual organisation of text and image (see, for example, Hochuli & Kinross 1996).

Psychologists use the term 'embodied reading', drawing on cognitive sciences and research. Accordingly:

> We do not only read with our eyes (not even in the most rigorous experimental setting). Neither do we write, text or tweet exclusively with our fingers and hands. All acts of human communication, creative expression, meaning construction, and learning convey the fact that, as human beings of a biological nature, our actions and interactions are inevitably and intrinsically multisensory. (Mangen & Schilhab 2012, 286)

However, embodied reading is not concerned merely with multisensory processes contained within the reader. The perspective takes inspiration from a recent shift in the cognitive sciences that goes under the name 'embodied cognition', an umbrella term used for the so-called 'four Es'; the mind embodied, embedded, enacted and extended (for example Menary 2010). Hence, embodied cognition breaks with the 'traditionalist' view that attributing meaning to words spoken and written occurs irrespective of the physical substrate, that is the body of the cognizer.

Inherent to the embodiment paradigm is instead the notion that humans are engaged in continuous interaction with and are therefore strongly embedded in their environments and the material present in them (Wilson 2002). As part of being alive, we instantaneously adjust and adapt to circumstances, environments and people (Schilhab et al. 2018). As such, our cognitive modus operandi is essentially malleable and volatile, which limits instances of amodal, abstract and arbitrary knowledge processing to select occasions (Schilhab 2017). Thus, the embodied reading view is sensitive to the complexity that constitutes reading situations, including their cultural meanings as these are played out in different historical settings and their replacement of traditional subject–object relations for many-faceted multi-level interactions, as well as their material composition.

Typographers are aware that the difference in materiality between printed and digital texts affects the reading experience. Paul Luna (2018) notes that e-books present a window of decontextualized text to the reader, denying them the insight that handling a physical book gives about the scope and overall structure of the work. Physical texts encourage kinds of reading that include turning back, looking forward, annotating and skipping, and regarding these activities e-book readers and software still fall short of the printed book. Materiality is also expressed by the physical, dimensional presence of letters, words and text on a page, and consideration of the processes by which they were put there. As noted by Eric Kindel,[1] this, in turn, brings about reading that blends material-sensory and cognitive aesthetics, and gives rise to reflections on the work of capturing thought and experience as language and (material) form.

We have organised the essays into three sections that represent the ways in which materiality was perceived in the COST workshops: where and how we read; the object of reading; and engaging with the text.

Theresa Schilhab and Anežka Kuzmičová explore how digital reading has transformed how and where people read, and relate this to grounded cognition. The late Paul Stiff's short paper (published in *Eye* magazine in 1993) questions the postmodern notion of the passivity of reading and the unconventional use of typography to make readers work to engage with

1 Informal correspondence with the editors in 2019.

a text, and that typography can affect how people read by addressing the needs of different kinds of reader and genres of text. Ana Vogrinčič Čepič, Patrícia Dias, Anežka Kuzmičová and Skans Kersti Nillson discuss how the reading device, type of text and purpose of reading relate to different bodily postures and physical environments, and the material advantages of the single-purpose nature of print books. Adrian Netedu reports on an empirical study about the role and place of reading in student daily activities in the context of student perspectives on the switch from printed books to digital resources.

Pasqualina Sorrentino, Massimo Salgaro, Teresa Sylvester, Jana Lüdtke, Arthur Jacobs and Gerhard Lauer address the dichotomy of digital native/digital immigrant, investigating the reading preferences and reading habits of younger and older people in relation to literary reading on paper vs. on screen.

Immersive reading presents an opportunity for reader–text interaction, shifting ideas about what is meant by the object of reading. *Alice in Wonderland* is used in Federico Pianzola and Wayne de Fremery's exploration of how a virtual reality reading (VR) environment might be designed to immerse the reader in the experience of the story, including sound and interpretations of landscape. In their visual essay, Chloé Aubry and Claire Gauzente propose a framework for studying the different material processes used in artists' books and their potential impact on the readers/users of such books.

The section on 'engaging with the text' is concerned with the ways different kinds of readers access content in printed and digital texts. Valeria Levratto discusses how accessing information in a text (conventionally done through indexes and contents pages in the case of a book, for example, which are produced by editors) has changed with digital formats, where readers are able to control routes through a text, and their individual interpretations of its content through tagging. A different perspective is given by Ann Marcus-Quinn and Triona

Hourigan, who explain how they encourage informal 'book making' to stimulate reluctant readers.

Based on their study with eye-trackers, Arūnas Gudinavičius and Andrius Šuminas discuss selecting strategies and browsing patterns among readers searching for books and query their accepted relation to age and gender. The anthology closes with an exemplary essay by Alenka Kepic Mohar, who reflects upon the shift in materiality of textbooks for education by examining several examples of primarily Slovenian textbooks from various periods, ending with digital versions.

References

Hochuli, J. & R. Kinross (1996). *Designing books: Practice and theory*, London: Hyphen Press.

Luna, P. (2018). *Typography: A very short introduction*, Oxford: Oxford University Press.

Mangen, A. & T. Schilhab (2012). An embodied view of reading: Theoretical considerations, empirical findings, and educational implications. *Skriv*, 285–300.

Menary, R. (2010). Introduction to the special issue on 4E cognition. *Phenomenology and the Cognitive Sciences*, 9(4), 459–463.

Schilhab, T. (2017). *Derived embodiment in abstract thought*. Cham: Springer.

Schilhab, T., G. Balling & A. Kuzmičová (2018). Decreasing materiality from print to screen reading. *First Monday*, 23(10), 1–12.

Wilson, M. (2002). Six views of embodied cognition. *Psychonomic Bulletin & Review*, 9(4), 625–636.

Acknowledgements

The chapter by Paul Stiff is reprinted form *Eye*, no. 11, 1993 by permission of Eye Magazine Ltd. The chapter by Alenka Kepic Mohar is reprinted from *LOGOS*, issue 2, 2019 with permission.

This publication is based upon work from COST Action IS 1404 E-READ, supported by COST (European Cooperation in Science & Technology).

Themes stem from discussions and meet ups in several European cities. We are grateful to Anne Mangen and Adriaan van der Weel for their vision and energy in setting up "Evolution of Reading in the Age of Digitisation" (E-READ), and their commitment to it.

We would like to thank our authors for their contributions and patience, the editorial office at Aarhus University Press, and Paul Luna who designed the book with impeccable attention to detail.

Where and how we read

Situated meaning-making and the places where we read

Theresa Schilhab & Anežka Kuzmičová

In recent years, a new cognitive research paradigm emphasising situated and bodily cognition has gained impetus. A growing number of neuroscience studies suggest that sensory-motor experiences shape the individual's development of concepts and language use. A commonly shared explanation of these findings proposes that when we as infants are acquiring language, linguistic activity is simultaneous with our perceptual access to the concrete phenomena and situations to which it refers. These situations become meaningful co-active 'sounding boards' that corroborate our competent language use. According to this theory, linguistic meaning invoked for example while reading occurs as a partial re-enaction of these situations. In this article, we highlight the implications of the close links between language and bodily situations in relation to reading in different places.

Grounded cognition

Every mental experience involves direct perceptual experiences. This claim is central to the field of 'Grounded Cognition' (hereafter GC), an overall term for cognitive and neuroscience theories that emphasise the situated and bodily bases of cognition (for example Barsalou 2010). In the CG approach, the immediate perception of our physical and social surroundings shapes both our behaviours and actions, and our linguistically articulated knowledge about the world.

In the CG perspective, learning builds on both exteroceptive sensations, such as sensory stimulation made available by and captured from the world outside the skin, and interoceptive sensations, such as sensory signals captured from within the body, as well as memory of past experiences (Barrett 2009). Direct experiences in the sense of immediate perception, which may involve both exteroceptive and interoceptive sources, form part of every learning experience.

However, the extent to which direct experiences contribute to a particular cognitive event differs depending on whether we engage in 'online' or 'offline' thought processes (Wilson 2002). In online cognition, direct experiences of concurrent phenomena, objects or events co-constitute the process. When you want to find a place to park your bicycle, you base your decision on the concurrent perception of the size of the bike and the dimensions of the parking space, as well as on earlier successful trials. Your online perception of the bicycle elicits activity in neurons that process different properties of the bicycle such as surfaces and edges, colour, sound and how it moves. Also, neurons sustaining affective reactions are active and may unwittingly contribute to your final decision.

In offline mentalising such as reading, direct experiences of online phenomena are seemingly less relevant. Here, the mental processes are based more on memory and interoception and less on online stimulation of the external senses. In understanding the dreams and hopes of the little match girl in the eponymous story by H. C. Andersen, for instance, one relies not on simultaneous perceptual experiences of the armchair supporting one's body but rather on consciously controlled imagination. It is the text-elicited mental images of the hungry child in the street peeping inside the homes of more fortunate others that primarily drives comprehension.

Situated language

The division between online and offline mentalising is not as clear-cut as it may seem, however. Based on brain scans and neurophysiological studies, contemporary cognitive science increasingly submits that the attribution of meaning to written or spoken language is due to the mind reenacting direct experiences rather than representing them in some purely disembodied way. This reenacting pertains to offline mentalising in general, including even abstract thinking (Schilhab 2017). Semantic meaning attribution while reading is thus a simulation of direct experiences as if they were immediate and experienced online.

The explanation for this is that, when acquiring language as infants, we have immediate perceptual access to the concrete phenomena and events to which the words – their sounds and articulatory qualities – refer. (Pulvermüller 2013). For instance, when pre-linguistic children are introduced to the concept 'dog', typically they are also experiencing an actual dog. The so-called neural correlate that emerges when acquiring the linguistic understanding of 'dog' therefore couples the sensory experience of the language processing, sounds and articulation, on the one hand, and the sensory-motor experience of a dog on the other. The neural correlate of 'dog' is thus comprised of numerous activations representing various sensory phenomena of which we are not normally aware, since they are not at the centre of our conscious focus – for example the dog's breathing, the physiology of its snout or the feel of its coat.

Thus, when children become competent language users reading 'dog', simultaneously they simulate previous sensations of real dogs by reactivating the neural correlate formed during previous direct experiences. The world and our words for it become meaningful as a result of continual associations between stimuli that originally elicited specific experiences. Once these are learnt, in the absence of the entire set of original stimuli the overall response may still be elicited automatically, but now by a much reduced set of stimuli.

Cognitive complexity

The influence of direct and bodily experiences on linguistic knowledge might not come as a huge surprise. After all, the remembrance of former vivid perceptions such as the scent of granny's kitchen or the taste of a childhood ice-cream in a particular location are common experiences (for example Schilhab et al. 2018). However, what seems surprising is how current perceptual experiences may impact on our mental processes in general. When we get a whiff of a particular odour, memories of previous circumstances corroborating the experience are immediately available to us although their urgent presence may appear somewhat dim.

Often the impact of our surroundings on our mental processes remains undisclosed to us. It has been shown that touching rough or soft surfaces of the pieces in simple puzzles influenced the subsequent assessment of social coordination in other people as either 'serious' or 'yielding'. Similar effects in evaluations of job candidates are induced by the use of heavy clipboards as compared with light. Even passive experiences of touch, by seating experimental subjects in either hard wooden or soft cushioned chairs, influenced the assessments of employees in an observed pretend conversation. In contrast to soft experiences, hardness primed participants to perceive others as less emotional, more stable, and less flexible in negotiation (Ackerman et al. 2010).

Within context-dependent memory research, it is known that environmental stimulation during a learning episode affects accessibility of memory during recall. In a renowned study, divers who learned arbitrary word strings on a beach and were later tested in a forced recall test either in the same environment or under water showed significantly better memory for the words in the congruent environment (Godden & Baddeley 1975).

Reading in different places

Given that the perceptual qualities of a place can influence cognitive processing, physical environments are of immediate relevance to learning and reading research. Obviously, when one's surroundings actively corroborate learning, perceptual and sensory-motor activities are included in the anchoring of one's understanding in a similar way to the infant learning about 'dog'. In outdoor schooling, for instance, objects, events and experiences are woven into the overall understanding. Outdoors mathematics teachers successfully convey the concept of volume by having students draw whales in the sand at the seaside and then lie down one after another until they fill up the outline. The seaside surroundings act as material anchors that aid in attending to and creating meaning in relation to the mathematical concept.

The effect of written text can also be enhanced when reading takes place in a locale or general context identical or similar to what is rendered in the text (for example Schilhab 2018). For instance, experimental evidence has shown that when a story is read in a story-congruent season of the year, readers are transported in the story world to a greater degree than when the same story is read in an incongruent season (Vaughn et al. Unpublished Manuscript). In such cases, environmental cues can serve to 'prop' one's mental imagery of the text's contents (Kuzmičová 2016). One's reading of *Moby Dick*, for instance, can acquire especially rich phenomenal qualities if read on the American East Coast, or in any other waterside location for that matter. The immediate proximity of water then potentially boosts the story's effect and meaning, regardless to some extent of how dissimilar one's actual setting may be from that of the story. The same applies to vivid memories (visual, olfactory, proprioceptive) of boat rides that may be triggered by the text; be they memories of a leisure cruise or of a proper fishing adventure, what primarily counts is their experienced personal resonance, rather than their 'factual' correspondence to the places and situations suggested by *Moby Dick*.

Conclusion

The current emergence of smartphones as the second most prominent reading device after printed books creates a new ecology where readers can potentially capitalise on situated meaning-making in a large variety of ways. Through their ubiquity and connectivity, smartphones and other mobile devices provide constant access to an unlimited wealth of texts, allowing one to read whenever and wherever, and to flexibly select content for optimal adherence to one's environment and situation. Moreover, dedicated mobile applications and experimental digital-born genres actively explore the potential of environmental propping by offering geolocative audio or textual feeds, a new 'outdoor literature' of sorts wherein the physical environment becomes purposefully integrated in the makeup of the text.

On the other hand, the bulk of reading experiences afforded by our more mundane mobile reading practices (Balling et al. 2019) do not seem particularly marked by text–environment congruence or situated meaning-making. Rather, mobile reading overall seems largely to level out many of the traditionally established associations between where and what we read. For instance, educational genres fostering specialist knowledge such as philosophical encyclopedia entries, previously reserved for the library or private study, are nowadays read in settings such as supermarket checkout lines or family dinners. These developments have potentially wide-ranging implications for the meaning we attribute to text when we read, and for the role played in text processing by our physical environment. As such they deserve a prominent place on future policy and research agendas.

References

Ackerman, J. M., C. C. Nocera & J. A. Bargh (2010). Incidental haptic sensations influence social judgments and decisions. *Science*, 328, 1712–1715.

Balling, G., A. C. Begnum, A. Kuzmičová & T. Schilhab (2019). The young read in new places, the older read on new devices: A survey of digital reading practices among librarians and Information Science students in Denmark. *Participations Journal of Audence & Reception Studies*, 16(1), 197–236.

Barrett, L. F. (2009). The future of psychology. *Perspectives on Psychological Science*, 4(4), 326–339.

Barsalou, L. W. (2010). Grounded cognition: Past, present, and future. *Topics in Cognitive Science*, 2(4), 716–724.

Godden, D. R. & A. D. Baddeley (1975). Context-dependent memory in two natural environments: On land and underwater. *British Journal of Psychology*, 66(3), 325–331.

Kuzmičová, A. (2016). Does it matter where you read? Situating narrative in physical environment. *Communication Theory*, 26(3), 290–308.

Kuzmičová, A., T. Schilhab & M. Burke (2018). m-Reading: Fiction reading from mobile phones. *Convergence*. 26(2), 333–349.

Pulvermüller, F. (2013). Semantic embodiment, disembodiment or misembodiment? In search of meaning in modules and neuron circuits. *Brain and Language*, 127(1), 86–103.

Schilhab, T. (2017). *Derived Embodiment in Abstract Language*, Cham: Springer Verlag.

Schilhab, T. (2018). Neural bottom-up and top-down processes in learning and teaching. *Postmodern Problems*, 8(2), 228–245.

Schilhab, T., G. Balling & A. Kuzmičová (2018). Decreasing materiality in print to screen reading. *First Monday*, 23(10), 1–12.

Wilson, M. (2002). Six views on embodied cognition. *Psychonomic Bulletin & Review*, 9(4), 625–635.

Stop sitting around and start reading

Paul Stiff

Postmodern typography sees the reader as an idler in need of short sharp shocks. But is reading really so passive a process?

Graphic designers used to have straightforward reasons for what they did. Paul Rand, for instance, could say, "If it looks terrific, then that's all I care about. After the looks, and strictly of secondary importance, comes client approval" (Woudhuysen 1989). Marcello Minale was equally clear: "The core of our philosophy is that design is based on self-expression".

As these simple credos have come to seem thin, more complex but equally designer-centred explanations have filled the vacuum. Michel de Boer of Studio Dumbar strikes a now-familiar note: "Design should not be too easy, either to do or to see. The receiver of the message should be made to work, forcing them to think about what they see" (Wood 1991). And if this disciplinarian injunction still sounds over-simplistic, more sophisticated versions are available. Michèle-Anne Dauppe has invoked "'the post-modern condition' and 'radical approaches to communication' which 'attempted to engage the audience with the text, to make the audience 'work', and to emphasise the 'construction' of meaning. Radical typography might aim not to flow seamlessly, legibly, but to halt and disrupt, to expose meaning and language as problematic" (Dauppe 1991). Rick Poynor suggests a Paris-Michigan lineage: "The Cranbrook theorists' aim, derived from French philosophy and literary theory, is to deconstruct, or break apart and expose, the manipulative visual language and different levels of meaning embodied in a design".

The visual style associated with these positions could (very loosely) be called 'postmodern deconstructed', or 'pomo' for short. The pomo claim is that reading is passive, uncreative, one-dimensional, and that readers are underchallenged, too lazy to discover that meaning is undecidable. Typographers should goad them to work – typically by removing familiar landmarks, by laying obstacles, diversions and false trails, and by recognising that "the cry of 'legibility' masks a reactionary attitude against progress, change or critical intervention" (Dauppe 1991).

The tone of these claims – of idlers in need of short sharp shocks – may sound familiar. But they pre-date both Thatcherism and pop deconstruction, and were made by book artists long before Barthes and Derrida featured in lifestyle pages. Joel Roth wrote in 1969 of a "new use of typography ... based on erratic type arrangement which pulls the reader in as an active participant, and makes reading a creative act rather than passive absorption of information" (Roth 1991, 193).

A variant on this theme is what Sharon Poggenpohl, editor of Visible Language, curiously calls 'content-responsive typography'. It is preferred in her journal because: "People read less, they obtain more of their information from other media ... contemporary readers who are distracted by more dynamic modes of presentation demand ... more responsive typography" (Poggenpohl 1991, 224–225).

These assertions deserve a response. First, there is little or no evidence to support them. The evidence we have about reading points to the contrary: that 'reading' is a highly complex set of activities, working on many levels – from the relatively automatic one of eye movements to the intentional levels of navigating, monitoring, sampling and selecting. When people read they make strategic choices, constantly generating inferences and hypotheses – about intention, relevance, tone of voice, and so on. Far from being passive and mechanical, reading is typically active and purposeful. (And all this is uncontroversially in line with post-modern theories of signifying practices which argue that each reading is a re-writing.)

Second, when pomos generalise about reading they often hide undeclared assumptions about what kind of readers they have in mind. They are less likely to imagine people deprived of literacy and its promises than a more comfortable fraction of the population favoured by designers as 'target audiences'. (What if readers are old, or visually impaired, or not very good at reading, or poor, or ignorant of their rights?) They rarely describe what kinds of reading form the object of designing, but seem to exclude educational texts, reports, forms, specifications, walkers' guides, catalogues, price lists, reference books, maps, diagrams, food and medicine labels, dictionaries, timetables, schedules, user manuals, and so on. Pomos appear to prefer something bracketed off within a more privileged 'literary' or 'artistic' category.

Third, 'content-responsive typography' – today justified as a response to the alleged demise of reading – seems little more than a new label for a well-worn rationalisation. Marinetti's hasty perceptions and screams do not need quotation here, but Vincent Steer may be less familiar. A founder of the British Typographer's Guild in the 1930s, he recommended that "a detective story might read more convincingly in a matter-of-fact typeface like Scotch Roman. A book intended to be read by a doctor or scientist might suitably be set in a precise and pedantic type like Bodoni Book, while a light novel ... would call for a more robust typeface" (Steer 1932).

Fourth, the tale of a lost golden age (once people read, now they watch videos) is here implicated with a competitive account of design, in which readers' choices are mediated by the free market. To survive the hazards of that market, messages have to be ostentatiously differentiated to draw attention to themselves, better to encourage readers to discriminate within an array of shopping opportunities.

Sceptics might ask: of all the sources of knowledge about reading and communication (cognitive psychology, ethnology, ergonomics, discourse analysis, feminism...), why have typographers defaulted to those which neither offer nor require evidence? To ones which permit them to 'theorise' reading as passive osmosis, to marginalise readers (mere receptacles) and at the same time to foreground the act of designing (explained as the 'challenging' of empty vessels)? Whose interests do such theories serve?

Although typographers may sprinkle their utterances with post-modern ferments (and perhaps, when business improves, the more expansive inflections of management-speak), their reflexes still draw them towards homelier territory. What could be more natural for young prizewinners than to describe their student days in epic terms: "It was very academic ... and it gave me an incredible grounding in type. But I had to fight to be creative" (Evamy 1991, 22). We know from Hollywood – remember Charlton Heston's *The Agony and The Ecstasy* and Kirk Douglas' *Lust for Life* – that it was ever thus.

Not much has changed. Once designers just wanted to look good; now they also want theories to justify looking good. To graduate into the creative elite they must first make a visibly personal mark. This designer-centred romance, which pomo designers share with Paul Rand and Marcello Minale, is endorsed by Hermann Zapf, who enthuses that "typographic creativity can be expanded ... as long as it is controlled by people with knowledge and taste" (Zapf 1987).

Designers' insensitivity to users is not unique to typography. Donald Norman reviews industrial design: "A good way to find out what the design world cares about is to read the magazines of industrial design. *ID* is a fascinating magazine, with clever innovative design. But I detect little interest in making design usable, functional, or understandable" (Norman 1988). And Ted Nelson, who put hypertext on our Macintoshes, is unimpressed by developments in design for interaction between people and computers: "It is nice that engineers and programmers and software executives have found a new form of creativity in which to find a sense of personal fulfilment. It is just unfortunate that they have to inflict the results on users" (Nelson 1990).

Critical reasoning about design has always offered alternative – modest but more challenging – forms of explanation. In 1968 the British Working Party on Typographic Teaching reported that inadequacies in design education arose mainly from treating the subject as "a form of personal visual expression ... Consequently, many unspectacular areas of design ... which play an important part in our lives are either not designed at all or are designed badly" (Working Party on Typographic Teaching 1968).

In 1970 Anthony Froshaug – practising, teaching and writing from the margins – reviews a showcase of 'pioneers': " 'Modern' typography is not a mode; it consists in a reasoned assessment of what is needed, and of what somehow is done, under certain constraints. When technical and social constraints change, the important thing is not to spray a random pattern on the page but to assess the new, with the old, requirements of the text" (Froshaug 1970).

Two decades later, in a final provocation, Otl Aicher argued that when "typographic signs become mere graphic material used as a kind of formal 'quarry' for symbols and textures ... then writing is reduced to nothing more than an aesthetic object" (Aicher 1988, 118).

Does any of this matter? Most graphic designers have managed to get by without explanations much more complicated than 'just do it'. But traditional graphic design has probably had its day, and is unlikely to survive – except perhaps as a 'heritage' craft – the more demanding questioning it now faces. The challenge for designers, still, is to explain. 'Because I like it this way and hope that other people will too' or 'because it expresses my feelings' may be fair explanations for relatively content-free designing. And while inadequate for design tasks which involve active readers with questions and purposes of their own, they at least have the virtue of honesty. What we are offered, in their place, is a mixture of personal preferences and designer-centred ideology. To elevate this to the status of a theory on design for reading is just another step on a false trail.

References

Aicher, O. (1993/[1988]). Typographie. *Eye*, 11(3), 118.
Dauppe, M. (1991). Get the message. *Eye*, 3(1), 4–7.
Froshaug, A. (1970). Typography ancient and modern. *Studie International*, 924, 60–61.
Evamy, M. (1991). The miller's tale. *Design Week*, 22.
Minale, M. (1989). *Design*, 489, 12.
Nelson, T. (1990). The right way to think about software design. In: B. Laurel (ed.), *The Art of Human-Computer Interface Design* (pp. 127–136), Reading, MA: Addison-Wesley.
Norman, D. (1988). *The Psychology of Everyday Things*, New York: Basic Books.
Poggenpohl, S. (1991). *Visible Language*, 25(4), 424–425.
Poynor, R. (1991). *Typography Now: The Next Wave*, London: Booth-Clibborn Editions.
Roth, J. (1969). Typography that makes the reader work. *Journal of Typographic Research*, 3(2), 193.

Steer, V. [no date: 1932?]. *Printing Design and Layout*, London: Virtue.
Wood, G. (1991). Too much legibility. *Desktop Publishing Commentary*, 7, 8–13.
Working Party on Typographic Teaching (1968). *Interim Report*.
Woudhuysen, J. (1989). Paul Rand hates logos. *Blueprint*, 37.
Zapf, H. (1987). *Hermann Zapf and his Design Philosophy*, Chicago: STA.

Books, comfort and discomfort

Observations from six focus group interviews

Ana Vogrinčič Čepič, Patrícia Dias, Anežka Kuzmičová & Skans Kersti Nilsson

This article explores the (dis)comforts of reading in print vs. digital formats. We ran a qualitative study with 36 student respondents across six countries and found that reading can be uncomfortable, but that physical discomfort is sometimes the reader's preferred choice. Based on our data we discuss how the reading device, type of text and purpose of reading relate to different bodily postures and physical environments. We conclude with a discussion of the material advantages of the single-purpose nature of print books.

Reading on different devices

Continuous reading is usually associated with bodily comfort. It is also often assumed that, along with increasingly efficient and practical reading devices, the activity of reading is becoming more and more comfortable: from the ancient scrolls that could only be read while supporting them with both hands to the much more convenient and easy to handle codex, first hardback, then paperback – and now the 'no-back' e-book materialized via various digital devices.

Computers, laptops, tablets, smartphones and dedicated e-readers all eliminate the book as a three-dimensional object. Even though the text per se is immaterial, its 'sinking' into an e-device seems to undermine its physical autonomy. This "lack of textual tangible presence" (Piper 2012) inevitably changes its status as a whole. It no longer exists on its own, but only together with other contents, communicated through the device. We are seldom alone with an e-text and e-reading is thus rarely just reading, since we are usually multitasking, perpetuating a state of continuous partial attention (Stone 2007).

Reading on a stationary computer means sitting behind a desk and is usually done at home, in a library, at school or at work. Laptops can be carried along and (when space and battery allow) used in cafés, on public transport, or in parks, while tablets and especially smartphones can be used practically everywhere, creating a zone of intimacy even in the midst of a subway crowd. Because smartphones are small and multi-purpose, their use is exploding worldwide.[1] Despite functioning primarily as devices for personal communication, or rather exactly because of it, their role as reading platforms is increasing.[2] With the most limited repertoire of services, dedicated e-reading devices are less widespread, and usually associated with more devoted and also older readers,[3] perhaps also because these gadgets most resemble a traditional book.

Throughout history, we can trace a progress towards lighter,

1 For 2018 the number of smartphone users is forecast to reach 2.53 billion. See statista.com/statistics/330695/number-of-smartphone-users-worldwide.

2 Pew research (September 2016) states that in the US, multipurpose devices (smartphones, tablet computers) are used more often than dedicated e-reading devices to access digital content: See www.cenveopublisherservices.com/blog/2016/9/7/pew-research-center-publishes-latest-findings-for-book-reading-2016.

3 Research shows that young adults are more likely to read e-books on their mobile phones than those over thirty (Baron 2015, 10).

smaller, more easily portable, cheaper, more inclusive reading devices with greater capacity. If 24 books of the *Iliad* took up 24 papyrus scrolls, one codex could easily encompass them all, while an e-reading platform can today store up to 6000 titles. Scholarly overviews of the evolution of reading tend to submit to a teleological story of a development from the awkward towards the effortless (Price 2004, 309). However, this story wrongly takes for granted that the most physically pleasant circumstances are always the reader's first choice. A closer look at how people actually read reveals that this is not necessarily the case. Below we present a cross-national study of students' reading practices that attests to a number of perceived advantages of discomfort.

Our study

Our findings are based on an exploratory study aiming to analyse reading practices and preferences across different technological devices. We conducted focus groups in Croatia (HR), Czech Republic (CZ), Portugal (PT), Slovenia (SI), Spain (ES) and Sweden (SE).[4]

The participants were 36 undergraduate and graduate students, the only criterion for participation being that they should be frequent readers and state that they enjoy reading. Their mean age was 21 and a half, and 21 were females. Most participants were enrolled in university programmes, but some attended professional training below university level. A wide range of subjects of study was represented, including anthropology, communication, economics, education, library

4 The study was conducted within the COST Action IS1404 E-READ project and was carried out by nine researchers: Anežka Kuzmičová (lead), Patrícia Dias, Ana Vogrinčič Čepič, Anne-Mette Bech Albrechtslund, André Casado, Marina Kotrla Topić, Xavier Minguez López, Skans Kersti Nilsson and Inês Teixeira-Botelho (see also Kuzmičová et al. 2017).

and information science, literature, modern languages, physiotherapy, social work, sociology, technology and theology. Students came from urban and rural backgrounds, some of them mentioning frequent or even daily commutes between their place of study and a rural home.

This multi-subject and multi-national design introduced a high degree of diversity and added some weight to any trends emerging across the groups.[5] There were six participants per session on average. The sessions took place between March and October 2016, and they lasted approximately an hour. Audio and/or video was recorded and later transcribed with anonymization of the participants.

The primary goal of the study was to explore the roles of a number of variables (purpose of reading, type of text and reading device) in selecting physical environments for reading, but in this article we focus on the question of how materiality in reading is experienced, evaluated and discussed. The act of reading will be interrogated to explore the materiality from an environmental point of view, mainly focusing on how embodied interaction, substrate affordances and ergonomic postures interact with environmental attributes experientially related to comfort and discomfort. Far from the discourse of a paper-free future, our participants revealed that each device serves different purposes for them, affording different bodily experiences in different types of environments.

The (print) book can be uncomfortable

Respondents across focus groups spontaneously mentioned various situations in which a reading device – either print or digital – can be experienced as clumsy and uncomfortable. Interestingly, many of these comments were directed at print,

5 Some variation attributable to cultural differences was observed, but it was difficult to generalize and was not something we focused on.

even though print was largely considered the only 'proper' means of reading and was in general absolutely preferred amongst all reading devices. Most commonly it was considered too heavy, but this referred mainly to bulky science fiction volumes with several hundred pages.

> Lying on your bed with a three hundred-page volume over you, it's very heavy. (PT5)

> When I read a printed book, I need to change posture more often. (ES4)

> My hand hurts, especially if it's a large book. (HR4)

However, while the print book was considered expressly 'uncomfortable' with reference to leisure reading, this is the type of reading which assumes the highest degree of comfort, pleasure and enjoyment, and is most often associated with the home environment in general and comfortable furniture (bed, couch, sofa) in particular.

The notion of comfort in reading is of course not limited to the strict physical handling of the reading device, but extends to other circumstantial and contextual elements of the reading experience. Our respondents often linked comfort to their general enjoyment of reading. They mentioned having their own particular rituals that help them achieve a higher level of comfort, even when they use devices that are not their favourite. For example, some participants mentioned taking off their shoes or tying up their hair before reading.

> When I'm studying in a public place and I want to read something personal while taking a break, I take off my shoes. It's a little gesture, but it changes the way I read. (ES3)

> If I have to read I tie up my hair. I associate that with relaxing. (ES2)

On the other hand, and quite to the contrary, playing with

one's hair while reading can also be perceived as relaxing, privileging e-books, since they are easier to handle with one hand:

> I'm used to fiddling with my hair when reading, so this is another reason to use the e-book. I can handle it with one hand. (ES4)

Reading pleasure can also be enhanced by 'external' factors, such as a specific type of light, weather, temperature, background noise and so forth. But when it comes to studying, comfort can become irrelevant or even disturbing.

Uncomfortable can be good

Our respondents do not always make their choices with the aim of maximum bodily comfort. Certain levels of bodily discomfort are sometimes deliberately chosen, depending on the purpose of reading. Leisure is usually associated with relaxed bodily postures that would be considered awkward in studying, which, on the other hand, is associated with upright postures.

> For pleasure I read on the sofa, in the armchair or in bed. When I read for my studies, I sit at the desk; I have to sit upright. (SE1)

> An article for the faculty I read at my desk, because [my desk] is reserved for my university stuff. However, when I take a book for pleasure I calmly lay down on the couch, I grab a cushion, a small blanket in the winter, and that's a wholly different posture. (ES2)

Our respondents strategically force themselves into upright positions and corresponding settings in order to regulate their attention.

> Fiction works fine in bed. Non-fiction would be difficult, I'd feel I'm not alert enough. I need a chair and desk or something. (CZ3)

> When I am reading for studying, I do it at my desk, and I use a pen. (PT6)

The purpose of reading also emerged as the main determinant in choosing specific forms of the book (print or digital in various formats and on various devices). Leisure is usually associated with print, while laptops and stationary computers were reported as a common study device and their limitations to bodily comfort were sometimes explicitly praised.

However, for notetaking as well as for a more intensive study experience, especially longer texts are sometimes printed and – it seems – would be printed more often if facilities were available and free of charge.

> It's super uncomfortable to underline on the computer. (ES1)

> I read research articles in PDF files directly on the computer rather than in print. I take notes in a special file. But when it comes to monographs, I have to read in print. (SE2)

These observations align with the findings of two recent meta-studies that summarized the results of empirical studies on differences between print and screen reading (see Singer & Alexander 2017 and Delgado et al. 2018), which in short reveal that comprehension is better when the text is read from paper, especially when it comes to non-narrative texts.

Also, non-dedicated settings, such as home and outdoors, were commonly associated with leisure, while studying is often reserved for dedicated settings such as libraries. Less comfortable technological devices, less comfortable bodily postures, and dedicated settings are strategically used as resources to increase concentration and to make studying sessions more effective.

> I really appreciate the constraints of the library ... It's both [temporal and spatial constraints]. Having the time slot certainly makes a difference, but it's mainly about this special environment that is so totally dedicated to reading ... I have several favourite libraries that I choose from depending on my mood. (CZ1)

Being bookish today

Finally, we would like to highlight an aspect of the print book that is accorded new meanings when our respondents have the option to choose from multiple reading devices: its single-purpose nature. In contrast to digital supports, which are inherently multi-purpose, print books cannot be used for much more than reading. Sticking with the p-book can therefore be interpreted as a statement, proving one's devotion to 'pure' reading activity. This means that books have gained an additional symbolic value, representing the primacy of this activity, and a true love for reading proper.

> I would never leave home without a book. (CZ5)

Although mobile phones are by all means a highly affective technology (Kuzmičová et al. 2018), they also prevent readers from manifesting their affection towards reading in general and to specific books in particular. For this very reason, multifunctional digital devices are sometimes perceived as contradictory to the image of a passionate reader, since others can never tell whether one is 'really' reading or just browsing on social media. This was a cause of concern for a parent of two:

> Since I have two little daughters, I don't like them to see me all the time with my mobile phone. I'm reading, but they don't know it. They don't know if I'm playing or reading or what I'm doing. I like to buy a book so that they can see me with the book in my hands. (ES1)

But it is, paradoxically, precisely the multi-purpose nature of digital devices that allows continuous reading in situations that are seemingly incompatible with reading activity, as in busy and uncomfortable settings or in other people's company.

> In digital, you read everywhere. It doesn't matter if you're on the bus or in class. (PT1)

Since using mobile phones in company is perceived as more socially acceptable than print reading due to its purportedly less immersive, and therefore less isolating, nature, our respondents sometimes use their mobile phones for reading unbeknownst to their social surroundings.

> That's why I prefer reading on my mobile, because not everyone can tell I am reading, they might think I'm scrolling on Facebook ... There would be a lot of comments in the classroom at school [if the participant's classmates knew she was reading fiction during recess]. (HR2)

Returning to the issue of comfort, it should be noted that more (physically) comfortable does not necessarily signify more pleasant. For many the absence of the scent component makes e-reading experience much less satisfying.

> I also think about the sensory impressions of holding a book. I don't think that e-books will ever smell. From a printed book there is a stream of scent coming up from the paper when turning pages. This is very important to me... (SE1)

Also, one could claim that being bookish means precisely insisting on reading regardless of the device or circumstance.

> If the book is very absorbing, my back hurts. (ES3)

Conclusion

The main outcome of our study is that readers manage the various aspects of reading, including its materiality and environmental context, strategically in accordance with their purposes and preferences. Putting the comfort and pleasures of reading aside, it is the practical aspect that often decides the choice of a reading platform – for example for a mother with a child sleeping in her lap the fact that smartphones enable reading in the dark can be decisive in choosing it over a print book. Readers thus constantly negotiate a number of issues in order best to manage their reading practices.

Studying is very obviously perceived as an activity different from reading for leisure. It clearly represents something more than 'just' reading, with 'just' standing for 'free', i.e. devoid of any particular intention, purpose or obligation. On the other hand, when you read for your studies, your reading is by default burdened by the fact that you will need to learn, understand and know what you have just read, and use it in one way or another, which gives the whole exercise an air of constraint. Studying is a kind of backstage, preparatory phase for some future performance. Being aware of this already takes away the liberty of unstructured reading according to one's own will and associates it with effort and some sort of subordination.

This doesn't mean that academic reading cannot be pleasurable, but pleasure is simply not its primary purpose. Above all it needs to be efficient. This is why it is often accompanied by little 'tricks' that sharpen one's attention and lessen one's comfort.

It is therefore crucial for dedicated settings such as libraries to keep some degree of traditional spatial organisation, including silent areas with hard chairs and desks for study purposes, as this seems to play a crucial role in facilitating a studious atmosphere. Reading is not a stereotyped activity, moulded by a single standard; it is diverse and it should be allowed and supported in its diverse forms. Readers do not play by a certain logically predictable set of rules. The way people read and what they do to make the most of their reading experience (either in terms of pleasure or knowledge) turns out to be a very creative practice.

Our study also shows how the materiality of reading readily plays a part in the preparatory phases of reading (Mangen &

van der Weel 2016), since the knowledge and culture built around print- and e-reading predetermine one's choice of device with regard to purpose. This is also why the implications of comfort and discomfort are hard to grasp. Our participants often seem to be morc comfortable with what they are used to. Even though familiar and comfortable do not mean the same thing, the effort required to get used to something new sometimes leads one to choose the physically less comfortable option. As one of our participants noted, backache is what marks a gripping book.

References

Baron, N. (2015). *Words Onscreen: The Fate of Reading in a Digital World*, New York: Oxford University Press.

Delgado, P., C. Vargas, R. Ackerman & L. Salmerón (2018). Don't throw away your printed books: A meta-analysis on the effects of reading media on comprehension. *Educational Research Review*, 25, 23–38.

Kuzmičová, A., T. Schilhab & M. Burke (2018). m-Reading: Fiction reading from mobile phones. *Convergence: The International Journal of Research into New Media Technologies*, 1–17.

Kuzmičová, A. et al. (2018). Reading and company: Embodiment and social space in silent reading practices. *Literacy*, 52(2), 70–77.

Mangen, A. &A. van der Weel (2016). The evolution of reading in the age of digitization: An integrative framework for reading research. *Literacy*,50(3), 116–124.

Piper, A. (2012). *Book was There: Reading in Electronic Times*, Chicago: University of Chicago Press.

Price, L. (2004). Reading: The state of the discipline. *Book History*, 7, 303–320.

Singer, L. M. & P. A. Alexander (2017). Reading on paper and digitally: What the past decades of empirical research reveal. *Review of Educational Research*, 87(6), 1007–1041.

Stone, L. (2007). Living with continuous partial attention. *Harvard Business Review*, 85(2), 28–29.

University students' reading and the use of digital resources and devices

Case study in Iași, Romania

Adrian Netedu

The global transformation of educational strategies and learning techniques implies a massive use of digital devices and the transition from printed to virtual learning resources. There is more and more social research on the impact of new technology on learning processes, development of certain skills, and dedicated leisure activities among university students. Within this context, the amount of time spent on the Internet and social networks has increased. The use of a large variety of devices and virtual resources has become common for all university students. We conducted a sociological study at the Alexandru Ioan Cuza University of Iași, Romania, regarding the role and place of reading in students' daily activities, and some of our questions were related to the students' views on the use of digital books and how they switch between printed books and digital resources. In this article, we will present some conclusions of this research.

Introduction

The transition occurring in reading habits from printed books to digital platforms is in full swing globally. The impact of these changes in the more general context of cultural consumption and in the field of education continues to constitute an important subject in sociological research. As regards the differences between printed books and e-books, Zhang and Kudva (2014) notice that "there is a need to understand whether they differ in function. If they fulfil the same functions in the same situational context, one may replace the other. However, if they do not, they may simply serve as complements to each other".

The future of the printed book is at the centre of many debates. While Carriere and Eco (2002) conclude that "this is not the end of the book", Gomez (2008) published a sensational title announcing *Print is Dead*. Carriere and Eco state that "the internet has returned us to the alphabet. The computer returns us to Gutenberg's galaxy; from now on, everyone has to read. In order to read, you need a medium". However, Gomez – whose view is more radical, judging by his title – specifies that "while relevance and popularity of printed material (such as books, magazines and newspapers) will get smaller and smaller over the next few decades due to digital reading, books themselves will never entirely go away". These general findings have become even more visible among university students, who constantly switch between traditional and digital contents. Large academic centres continue to hold significant volumes of books in print media, while offering increasing amounts of digital material.

Rockinson-Szapkiw et al. (2013) studied the differences that occur in the learning process when using electronic sources as opposed to traditional ones (printed). One of the important conclusions of this research was that the electronic textbook is as effective for learning as the traditional textbook, and "the students who chose e-textbooks for their education courses had significantly higher perceived affective learning and psychomotor learning than students who chose traditional printed textbooks". At the opposite pole, we recall another study (Carvalho et al. 2019) conducted at the University of Extremadura in Spain (academic year 2017–2018) in which it was noticed that "the largest number of university students continues to prefer to study from printed books", one of the justifications being that "reading on paper allows reaching higher levels of concentration".

In another study, Karsenty (2014) lists 25 advantages of digital books, grouped by categories: cognitive, affective, social and other. The author emphasises the fact that high school students (selected from Canadian schools) using different devices can read a variety of texts in a modern societal context where young people read less and less printed books. In this context, says Karsenty, youth should be encouraged to read something other than Facebook pages, text messages and tweets.

Starting from the suggestions of these previous studies (some of which are presented in this introduction), we decided to conduct sociological research on a representative sample of students enrolled at the Alexandru Ioan Cuza University of Iași, Romania, in order to answer the following questions: To what extent do university students endorse digital documents? To what extent do students consider traditional books (in print) likely to disappear? What are the perceived advantages and disadvantages of reading digital books? Finally, we constructed a statistical index with which we tested a number of statistical assumptions.

Methods: participants, instruments

To begin, we present some information about the Alexandru Ioan Cuza University. The official website states that it is the oldest higher education institution in Romania, founded in 1860. It educates over 23,000 students at a time within its fifteen faculties. The great majority of these students can use the services and infrastructure of the 'Mihai Eminescu' Central University Library, which holds over 2,500,000 printed volumes, and collaborates with similar institutions all over the world for its documentation. From this great library, university students and academic staff have free access to extensive databases of scientific articles and e-books.

The research presented in this article was carried out in May 2017 at the Alexandru Ioan Cuza University with master's students enrolled on the Public Relations and Publicity programme as field operators. We sent questionnaires to a target population of bachelor's students. Sampling units were whole student groups chosen randomly after a prior stratification; we used probabilistic, stratified, clustered samples. The volume of the sample was 963 students, the maximum error ±3.2% and the confidence level 95%. The sample structure was established following three variables: gender (35% male, 65% female); study domains (Exact sciences 9.1%, Natural sciences 13.5%, Humanistic sciences 10.3%, Theology 5.3%, Law 13.3%, Sociology/politics 18.9%, Economics 27%, Sports 2.6%), and year of study (first year 37%, second year 35%, third year 25%, and fourth year 2%).

The use of different reading devices

Our aim was to describe some of the important social representations surrounding printed and digital books, the use of different reading devices, and perceptions of the advantages or disadvantages of using digital devices.

Most university students are convinced that printed books will not disappear (70%), while 27% consider that printed books will gradually disappear (see Figure 1).

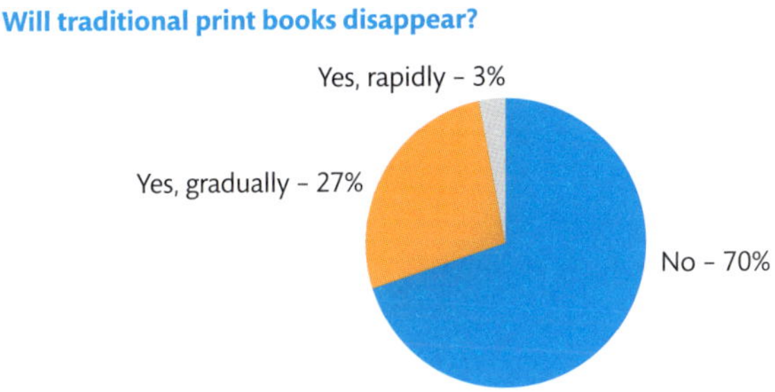

Figure 1 Whether traditional textbooks will disappear

In our research, only 52% of the respondents declared that they regularly read digital books or articles. Among them, the use of specific devices is both very diverse and predictable (see Table 1).

Table 1 Percentage reading digital books or articles

	Yes	*No*
Do you use an e-reader (for example a Kindle)?	8%	92%
Do you read on your desktop computer/laptop?	46%	54%
Do you read on your tablet/phone/smartphone?	40%	60%
Have you bought digital books in recent years?	10%	90%
Do you have a subscription with a virtual library?	11%	89%

We notice that the use of e-readers is very limited due to the associated costs, but the university students prefer handy reading devices (computers or phones), even if they do not have specific reading facilities like dedicated e-readers. This kind of 'digital consumption' is shown in a graph of the principal component analysis (see Figure 2).

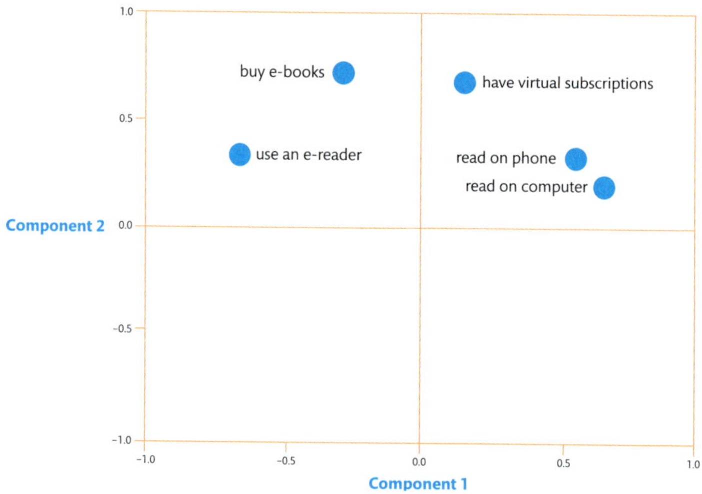

Figure 2 Use of digital devices

We noticed that 'the use of an e-reader' was opposed to practices of reading using handy devices. Buying e-books is related to subscriptions to virtual libraries.

With the five dichotomous variables quoted above in Table 1, we constructed a statistical index called 'digitalopen'. This is a cumulative statistical index calculated with a 'count values' procedure, which can have a score between zero and five points (each positive answer received one point and a 'higher degree of acceptance of digital reading use' means that a subject chose affirmative answers for all five variables). Descriptive statistics of this index with 501 available cases is represented in Table 2.

Table 2 Descriptive statistics for the 'digitalopen' index

	N	*Minimum*	*Maximum*	*Mean*	*Mode*	*Standard Deviation*
'digitalopen' index	501	0.00	5.00	2.129	2.00	0.94506

With this statistical index we tested the hypotheses H1 and H2:

H1. There are significant differences in openness to the use of digital devices for reading, depending on a student's gender, specialisation and year of study. We split this hypothesis into three other hypotheses:

H1a. There are significant differences in openness to the use of digital devices for reading depending on a student's gender. Using the Mann Whitney Test, we noticed that there were no significant differences in openness to using digital devices according to gender ($U=27919.5$, $N1=171$, $N2=330$, $p=0.838$).

H1b. There are significant differences in openness to the use of digital devices for reading depending on a student's specialisation. In this case, we recoded the variable study *domains* into two categories: (1) exact or natural sciences and economic specialisations, named hereafter *scientific*, and (2) other specialisations. In this case, the percentage became 49.6% (scientific specialisations) and 50.4% (other specialisations). With the Mann Whitney Test, we noticed that there were no significant differences in openness to using digital devices based on the two categories of specialisation ($U=30766$, $N1=247$, $N2=254$, $p=0.649$).

H1c. There are significant differences in openness to the use of digital devices for reading based on a student's year of study. Using the Kruskal Wallis Test, we noticed that the scores for openness to using digital devices for reading in the four conditions of 'year of study' do not differ significantly ($\chi^2=2.69$, $df=3$, $p=0.441$).

In conclusion, hypotheses H1a, H1b and H1c were not confirmed.

H2. The opinion on the disappearance of printed books is associated with reading digital books or articles. From our data, we conclude that there is a significant association between the cited opinion and reading digital books or articles ($\chi^2=10.47$, df=2, p=0.005). The students who do not read digital books believe to a greater extent that printed books will not disappear.

We tested one final hypothesis (which adds two subhypotheses):

H3. The time spent on the Internet or on social networks is associated with an increased tendency to read digital books.

From our data, we concluded that there was no significant association between the amount of time spent on the Internet and reading digital books ($\chi^2=5.03$, df=2, p=0.08). In the second case, we concluded that there was a significant association between the time spent on social networking sites and reading digital books ($\chi^2=12.63$, df=2, p=0.002). These results need to be further investigated in qualitative research, because we expect that in the first case there was also a significant association.

Reading printed books vs. reading or buying e-books

It is important to remember that we can distinguish between e-books as electronic copies of traditional books or PDFs, and e-books available exclusively in a digital format (books only published on the Internet, virtual media etc.). Rockinson-Szapkiw et al. (2013) called these two types of e-books “fidelity e-textbooks” and “reflowable digital e-textbooks”. Other authors distinguish between ‘digital resources’ and ‘e-books’. Perhaps some confusion between these two types of digital resources is normal for the respondents in our research, but we consider that distinguishing e-books from other digital content does not raise interpretation problems. The difference between the use of electronic and traditional print textbooks can be seen in Table 4.

Table 3 Students' reading in the last year

	Fewer than 5	*Between 5 and 9*	*More than 10*	*None*
(*a*) How many printed books have you read?	41%	30%	24%	4.5%
(*b*) How many printed books have you bought?	47%	20%	18%	14%
(*c*) How many e-books have you read?	41%	14%	9%	36%
(*d*) How many audiobooks have you bought?	21%	3%	2%	70%
(*e*) How many books have you borrowed from the library?	31%	24%	26%	18%
(*f*) How many books have you bought from virtual libraries (Elefant, Libris, Emag, etc.)?	36%	17%	12%	34%

In this table, the percentages up to 100% represent non-responses. The data from this table are significant for an academic space dominated by printed books. Reading practices are relatively frequent, which can be explained by the preoccupations and intellectual character of the target population. However, considering the fact that such questions are connected to issues of individual prestige, the percentages should be viewed with caution.

Advantages and disadvantages of reading digital books

Reading digital books or articles can raise many problems related to adaptation, accessibility and personal health. In an open question, we identified some categories of responses with the highest frequency (see Table 4).

Table 4 Advantages and disadvantages of reading digital books

Advantages	*Disadvantages*
Accessibility	Sight impairment
Storage capacity	Dependence on power supply
Easy to carry	Reliance on an Internet connection
There are many free e-books	Reading becomes exhausting
Convenience	Missing the 'physical' book
Low cost (compared to prices of printed books)	The tendency to browse (the sense of lack of reading depth)
Ecological	

The actual responses were much more diverse and detailed. For example, the emphasis on the ecological dimension involves more comments on the physical production of printed books through the use of natural resources. It is worth noting that a number of respondents associate digital reading devices with a reduced predisposition to in-depth reading.

Conclusion

In our exploratory research, we have tried to identify some features of digital consumption among university students. Our questionnaires covered the wider theme of reading consumption practices (irrespective of their purpose). The results are valid only on the built-in sample with inferential relevance to the population of bachelor's students from the university.

Certainly, the results would be very different if the educational institution studied had a technical or medical specialisation.

In our research we tested three hypotheses. We did not find any significant differences in openness to the use of digital devices for reading according to students' gender, specialisation or year of study. In a second hypothesis, we proved that students who do not read digital books believe to a larger extent that printed books will not disappear. In the third hypothesis, we concluded that there was a significant association between the time spent on social networking sites and reading digital books.

In what follows, we add some descriptive results on the reading practices of university students and on the advantages or disadvantages of reading digitally.

In our opinion, this kind of research can be useful for institutional staff or administrations to improve student relationships with digital resources, to expand access to such resources and to avoid unauthorised downloads from the Internet. In-depth research could then be carried out in accordance with each specialisation, as there may be specific requirements either for individual study or for the development of a thematic infrastructure. It is safe to say that digital resources would be used more often if their cost were lower. Further research could focus on all five universities from Iași to get representative samples for each of the educational units.

References

Carriere, J. C. & U. Eco (2002). *This is Not the End of the Book*, London: Harvill Secker.

Carvalho, J. L., R. L. González, L. M. Casas García & J. C. Juarez (2019). What is better to study: The printed book or the digital book? An exploratory study of qualitative nature. *Computer Supported Qualitative Research. WCQR 2018. Advances in Intelligent Systems and Computing*, vol. 861, Cham: Springer.

Gomez, J. (2008). *Print is Dead: Books in Our Digital Age*, New York: Macmillan.

Karsenti, T. (2014). 25 principaux avantages du livres numériques. Online at karsenti.ca.

Rockinson-Szapkiw, A. J., J. Courduff, K. Carter & D. Bennett (2013). Electronic versus traditional print textbooks: A comparison study on the influence of university students' learning. *Computers & Education*, 63, 259–266.

Zhang, Y. & S. Kudva (2014). E-books versus print books: Readers' choices and preferences across contexts. *Journal of the Association for Information Science and Technology*, 65(8), 1695–1706.

Does age determine whether we read e-books?

Questioning the dichotomy of digital natives vs. digital immigrants

Pasqualina Sorrentino, Massimo Salgaro, Teresa Sylvester, Jana Lüdtke, Arthur Jacobs & Gerhard Lauer

The dichotomy 'digital native/digital immigrants' was introduced in 2001 by Mark Prensky with the aim of describing the digital divide existing between young people and the elderly. The metaphor has had enduring influence on how the educational system perceives students and technology. Most scholars do not like it, for various reasons. Among other problems, the term implies that technological abilities are innate rather than taught and learned. The purpose of this study is to examine whether there is any empirical evidence to support the use of the metaphor. We looked at the reading preferences and habits of younger and older people in relation to literary reading on paper vs. on screen. We tested subjects (n = 59) of different ages and socio-cultural backgrounds. Our results clearly distinguish between two attitudes towards literary reading on screen, represented by readers who have been using a digital device for longer than three years, and readers who have used one for no longer than two years or who have never handled one.

Introduction

It is often stated that we are living in an era of a great cultural transformation: the third "reading revolution" (Darnton 1991, 148). After the invention of writing 6,000 years ago and of the Gutenberg printing press in the 15th century, the introduction of digital texts and reading devices such as the Kindle in 2007 has changed our reading minds again (Wolf 2007). Along with the embodiment and diffusion of digital technologies into every part of our society and economy, a whole new generation of young people was born: the so-called digital natives.

Marc Prensky (2001), working in the field of education, introduced the dichotomy of digital natives/digital immigrants in order to describe a generational divide. According to Prensky's classification, the first group are the 'native speakers' of the digital language of computers, the Internet and video games – the generations who were born into the digital world. The so-called 'digital immigrants', on the other hand, are represented by those who started to use the language of new technologies at a later stage in life, and "like all immigrants, some [learn] better than others – to adapt to their environment, they always retain, to some degree, their 'accent', that is, their foot in the past" (Prensky 2001).

The debate about digital natives is heated (Bennet et al. 2008). Scholars do not agree on the terminology employed to identify this new generation, nor on their exact age range. 'Net Generation' (Tapscott 1997), 'Generation Y', 'Millennials'

(Howe & Strauss 2000), 'Digital Natives' (Prensky 2001) and 'iGen' (Twenge 2017) are all competing terms used in the digital natives literature. According to Johnson and Johnson (2010) digital natives are those who were born between 1981 and 1995 (Johnson & Johnson 2010). Smola and Sutton (2002) argue that the digital natives are those born between 1979 and 1994. For Tapscott (2009) the digital natives are those born between 1977 and 1997.

An additional problem when it comes to research on literary reading on screen versus on paper (Dillon 1992; Ziefle 1998; Mayes et al. 2001; Wästlund et al. 2005; Noyes & Garland 2008; Mangen & Kuiken 2014; Mangen, Walgermo & Brønnick 2013) is that the subjects of investigations are usually students – who are, according to Prensky, digital natives. It is therefore questionable whether the results of such studies could be generalized.

Theoretical background

Before 2007, when Amazon launched the first Kindle, the word 'book' was always associated with something physical – with specific paratextual information (Genette 1997) given by typography, cover, size and colour. Due to the long Christian tradition of book production and the close ties between bourgeois society and printing culture since the 18th and 19th century, in the 20th century the culture of books in the Western world turned into a new cult of books: dictators' publications became the 'sacred' core of state propaganda and a tool for the manipulation of the people (Koschorke 2016).

For historical and biographical reasons, different readers developed various attitudes towards books and screens. Especially for the older generation, the book was something 'sacred'; it had its own 'materiality' and 'originality'. Already the concept of 'original' has been severely compromised by the invention of printing. "Yet the digital media has marginalized the notion of the original even further.... After all digital copies cannot be distinguished from the original" (van der Weel 2011, 181–182). All digital texts, regardless of provenance or quality, look identical.

Literary reading is a human–technology interaction that involves our bodies and our brains engaging with a device of certain ergonomic and audio-visual affordances. In addition, the book has a user interface (i.e. cover, paper, titles, page numbers) according to van der Weel (2011, 187), but we are so used to it that we do not notice it anymore. Digitalization can implicate haptic changes, such as the way we interact with different media with our hands. When we read on an e-reader, we click and scroll through the pages, while in paper reading we are literally in touch with the text itself (Mangen 2008, 405). In a recent study of iPad apps in kindergarten, Merchant (2015) found that the body and in particular the hands are fundamental when using iPad apps for story-reading with young children. The haptics of the iPad interface makes a crucial difference for meaning-making, for the experience of stories, for navigation through the text and for how the texts are shared overall (Merchant 2015). These haptic differences were also tested in previous experiments. For example, Mangen and Kuiken (2014) wanted to examine the effects of reading medium (iPad vs. booklet) and a paratext manipulation (fiction vs. nonfiction) on aspects of narrative engagement. Their results indicated that subjects using the iPad reported uncertainty about location within text (dislocation) and a poorer grasp of its length.

This finding replicates evidence from other studies indicating that readers lose their sense of where they are in the text when reading on screen (Piolat et al. 1997; Wästlund et al. 2005; Mangen et al. 2011; Walgermo & Brønnick 2013). The most interesting main effect was for the measure of medium awkwardness, in that subjects reading non-fiction on the iPad reported feeling that the holding and manipulation of the medium was more awkward during reading than readers in the booklet condition (sample items: "I felt awkward manipulating the booklet/iPad during reading"; "I felt awkward holding the booklet/iPad during reading").

Starting from Prensky's dichotomy, the aim of the current study is to investigate whether the categories of digital natives, namely the younger generations born into the digital world, and digital immigrants, those who started to use new technologies at a later point in their life, exist in relation to reading habits associated with literary reading on paper vs. on screen. Furthermore, it explores possible differences between the two groups. We want to see whether there is any empirical evidence to support the use of Prensky's metaphor of digital natives vs. immigrants in the first place, questioning its usefulness in characterising particular generations of people.

Methods

Fifty-nine participants (37 women, 22 men) aged between 18 and 70 years old (M age=40.0, SD age=18.8) were recruited in the area around Göttingen and Berlin through printed and online advertisements, and social networking websites (i.e. Facebook). Forty-nine participated for free; the remaining ten were volunteers who participated for compensation. All of them were from different backgrounds: there were workers, pensioners, and people with and without academic educations.

The first part of the study enabled all participants to experience the reading of different pieces of literature in paper books and on an electronic device (Kindle reader). All participants read two short stories and two poems, one each in a paper book and on the Kindle reader, in a counterbalanced order. After reading each text, participants filled out some memory tests and rated their agreement with a list of statements regarding their reading experience on a 5-point scale.[1] At the end of the study participants filled out an additional questionnaire. Besides the questions related to their age, gender and educational achievement, they responded to the items presented below concerning their reading habits:

1. How many years have you been reading digitally in your free time?
   Answers on a 5-point scale: 1 (for more than 5 years) – 5 (never)

2. How many books did you read last year in your free time?
   Answers on a 5-point scale: 1 (more than 20) – 5 (none)

The first two questions regarding the subjects' familiarity were used to split the sample into two groups independently of their age and focusing on their digital reading experience. To explore group differences due to familiarity with digital texts further, we also presented an adapted form of the haptic dissonance scale (Gerlach & Buxmann 2011). Participants indicated their agreement with the following statements on a 5-point rating scale (from 1, I strongly disagree, to 5, I strongly agree):

3. For me it makes no difference whether I read a printed book or an e-book.

4. I find reading in digital formats cold.

5. An e-book is more technical and reminds me of work.

6. Reading an e-book feels more technically distant and not natural in my hands, thus I cannot establish a close relationship with the book.

7. Paper books for me have a kind of 'fragrance'.

8. I set a high value on the paper quality of printed books.

1 For more information regarding the items adopted, see Salgaro et al. (2018).

To test whether both groups corresponded to the assumed Prenskyian dichotomy of digital natives/digital immigrants, we compared the answers of both groups to all other questions about their reading habits and their usage of digital vs. paper texts for leisure reading (described below):

9. Do you prefer to read digital or printed books in your free time?
   Answers on a 5-point scale: 1 (only digital books) – 5 (only printed books)

10. Which medium supports deep reading (better)?
    Answers on a 5-point scale: 1 (only digital) – 5 (only printed)

Results

As a first step, we used item 1, concerning familiarity with the digital medium, to split the participants into two groups. Thirty-three participants (66.7% female) reported a high familiarity, indicating the usage of digital media for leisure reading for more than three years. The remaining 26 participants (57.7% female) reported low familiarity, indicated by no usage of digital devices (or usage for less than 2 years).

Comparing both groups with respect to age indicated no significant differences: $t(57) = 1.7, p = 0.10$. As shown in Figure 1, we could identify young participants below 40 reporting less familiarity (measured in time spent reading digitally in their free time), as well as older participants reporting high familiarity.

This outcome is interesting because it suggests that neither young nor elderly people are homogeneous in terms of their use of technologies for reading. In accordance with other studies (Helsper & Enyon 2008; Herring 2008; Cheong 2008), our findings seem to reject this idea of digital expertise and technological savviness based on date of birth. Furthermore, we did not register any differences between the groups in term of reading frequency, since our subjects reported the same amount of

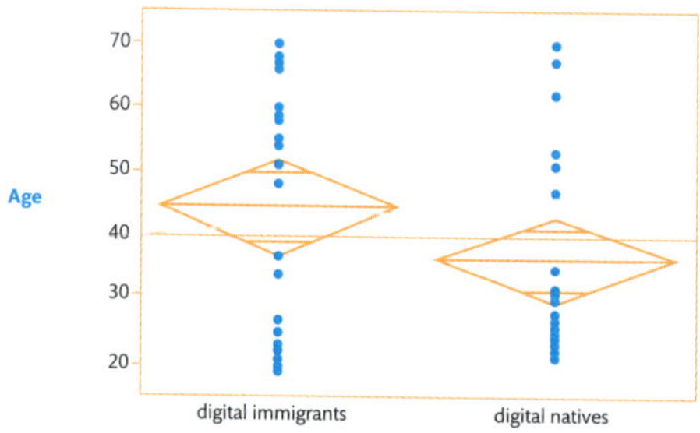

Figure 1 Responses to 'How many years have you been reading digitally in your free time?', revealing age distributions of digital immigrants and digital natives among participants

Note: Each error bar is constructed using a 95% confidence interval of the mean

leisure reading in response to item 2 ($\chi^2 = 1.4$, $p = 0.8$). For the remainder of this chapter, we therefore use the labels low vs. high familiarity to refer to both groups.

To explore the two familiarity groups further, we compared whether they see any differences in reading paper books compared to reading e-books (item 3). The high familiarity group agree more strongly with the statement that reading paper books does not differ from reading e-books than the low familiarity group, shown in the t-test: $t(57) = -2.7$, $p = 0.009$.

The results presented in Figures 2–4 show that familiarity with the medium determines whether digital reading was perceived as 'cold', 'distant' and/or associated with work (items 4–6). Compared with the high familiarity group, members of the low familiarity group perceived e-books as 'cold', $t(57) = 4.2$, $p = 0.0001$, as associated with work (t-test: $t(57) = 3.9$, $p < 0.001$) and as distant (t-test: $t(57) = 4.5$, $p < 0.0001$). Readers from the low familiarity group were not able to establish an emotional, close connection with texts in an e-book format. For literary reading, this is an important gap as it seems emotional bonding with the fictional characters is impeded by the digital medium. Gerlach and Buxmann (2011) described this lack of (warm) haptic feeling as "haptic dissonance".

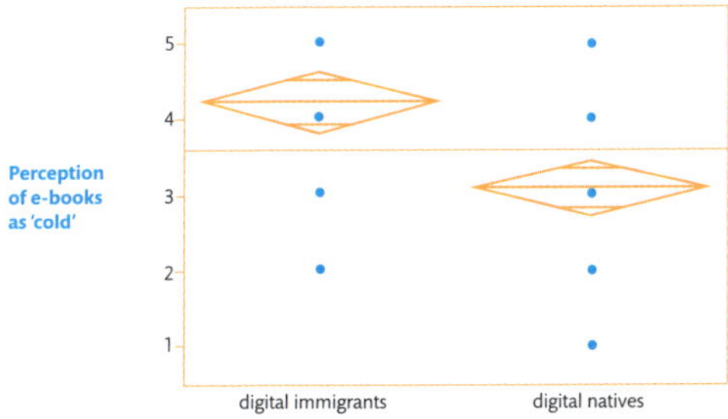

Figure 2 Responses to the statement 'I find reading in digital formats cold'
Note: Each error bar is constructed using a 95% confidence interval of the mean

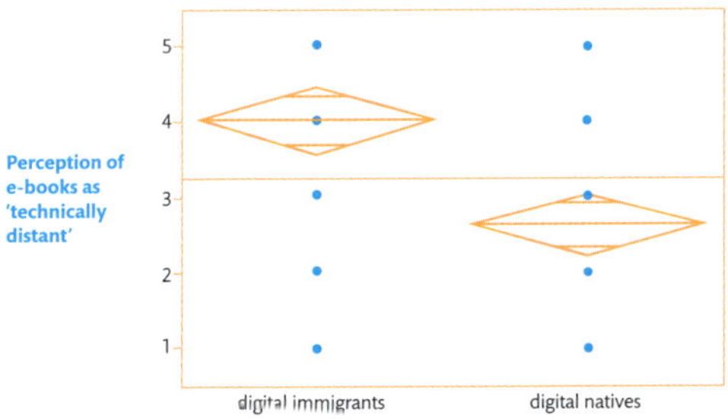

Figure 3 Responses to the statement 'Reading an e-book feels more technically distant and not natural in my hands, thus I cannot establish a close relationship with the book'
Note: Each error bar is constructed using a 95% confidence interval of the mean

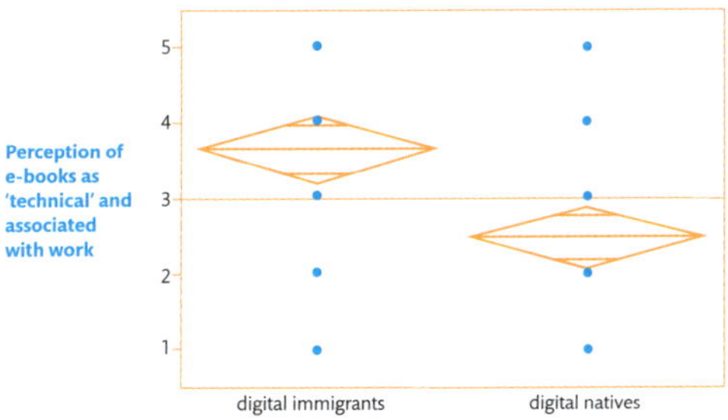

Figure 4 Responses to the statement 'An e-book is more technical and reminds me of work'
Note: Each error bar is constructed using a 95% confidence interval of the mean

Moreover, subjects with a low e-reading familiarity also perceived the e-book as more technically distant and not natural in their hands. It seems that they struggle to establish a close relation with e-books. This is in line with the assumption that texts presented in paper books are often described as tangible, whereas texts presented on screen are described as *intangible* and *detached* or *mediated* (Mangen 2008). Our data show that people who are unfamiliar with digital devices in particular differ in their perceived materiality of text on paper and of text on a screen. It is important to highlight the exact phrasing of the description of these embodied sensations, as digital texts are described as "distant" and "not natural", which refer to precise bodily sensations.

Reading on paper seems to be related to a kind of emotional state of mind that leads readers with low digital familiarity to perceive mechanical devices as an obstacle to building a close relation with a book.

Furthermore, the results related to the acceptance of the medium showed that e-reading, far from being a leisure activity, was perceived by the low familiarity group as technical and associated with work. Again, the familiarity with the medium compromises the perception that the subjects have of the reading experience as a moment of relaxation and enjoyment. It seems that subjects naturally distinguish between reading for leisure on paper and reading for work digitally, where literary reading belongs to the first activity.

Additional analysis indicated that the familiarity groups differ especially in their perceptions and evaluations of e-books. As shown in Figure 5, the groups do not differ significantly (both $t<1$) in their evaluations of the materiality of reading paper books (items 7–8). Both groups agreed equally strongly with the statement that paper books have a kind of 'fragrance' and that paper quality is important.

The findings presented in this study suggest that the di-

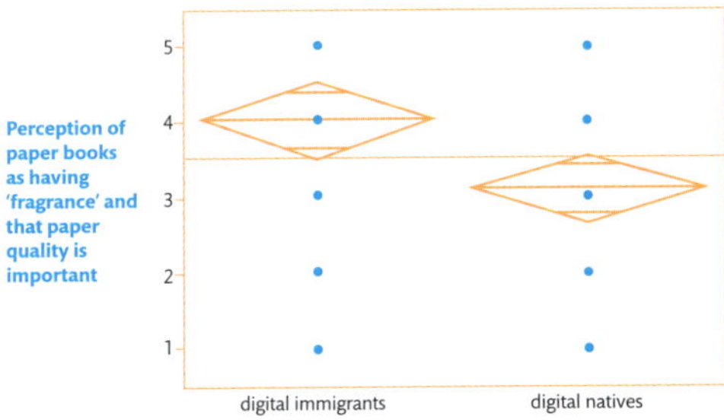

Figure 5 Responses to the statements 'Paper books for me have a kind of "fragrance"' and 'I set a high value on the paper quality of printed books'
Note: Each error bar is constructed using a 95% confidence interval of the mean

chotomy of digital natives/digital immigrants when related to reading behaviour (paper vs. screen) is misleading. The inconsistency of the Prenskyian dichotomy with respect to literary reading in free time is further revealed by the findings represented in the following graph in respect to the preferred medium for leisure reading. According to our results, not only the low familiarity group, but also the high familiarity one showed a stronger inclination for reading printed books rather than digital ones in their free time (item 9, Figure 6).

The paper book is preferred by subjects in both groups as the medium allowing an active process of thoughtful and deliberate reading, or "deep reading" (Wolf 2009), which supports comprehension including critical analysis, reflection and insight (item 10, Figure 7). These results evidence the social prestige associated with the printed book in Western culture, a culture described by Adriaan van der Weel as based on the "Order of the Book" (van der Weel 2011), and shed light on a prejudice against digital media which is not empirically based, since in our study we did not register any difference in comprehension and memory across reading media.[2]

2 See Salgaro et al. (2018) for further results.

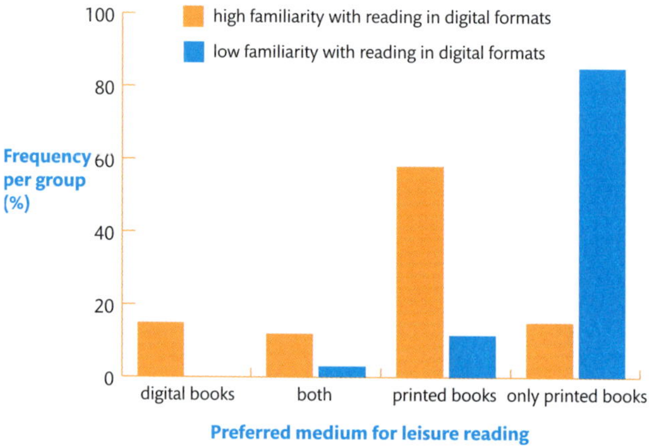

Figure 6 Responses by group to the question 'Do you prefer to read digital or printed books in your free time?'

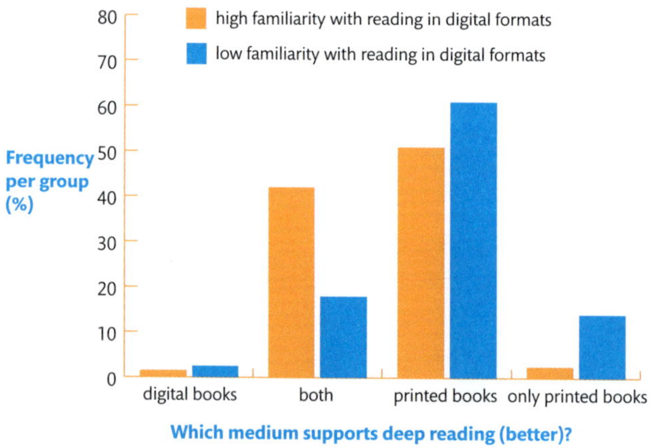

Figure 7 Responses by group to the question 'Which medium supports deep reading (better)?'

Overall, our results show that familiarity with a reading medium is crucial in determining the quality of people's reading experience. Haptic dissonance is the result of a mismatch between the familiarity of the reader with the medium and the medium itself.

Conclusion

Our findings reject popular generational stereotypes according to which young is equivalent to digitally or technologically adept, and the existence of a "digital divide" (Compaine 2001), or a gap between people with effective access to digital technology for leisure reading and those with very limited or no access at all. In line with other studies, our results reinforce the critique of the age-associated notions of "digital natives" and "digital immigrants" (Bennet et al. 2008).

At least for our subjects, it was not age, but preference and familiarity with the digital medium that were the discriminating factors. This supports previous findings (Chen et al. 2014; Margolin et al. 2013; Noyes & Garland, 2003) on the correlation between subjects' reading performance on screen vs. on paper and their familiarity with the reading medium.

The value of the physicality of reading – the importance of touch – seems to be a key aspect in explaining the different reading preferences of the two groups. Finally, both the printed book and the e-reader are objects that offer specific affordances and therefore haptic interactions.

The study's outcome contributes to the discussion on literary reading on screen vs. on paper. Along the same lines as other similar studies, our results seem to indicate that the paper book still has an important position in our society and that e-books are not taking over.[3]

Unlike some previous studies, however, it allows generalization of the results to various kinds of literary readers, since the interviewed sample included different ages and varied

3 See Delgado et al. 2018.

backgrounds. The experiment was focused on personal experience and comprehension but did not distinguish between learning and remembering. A further limitation of this study is the limited number of participants. To make more general statements about the dichotomy of digital immigrants/digital natives a test including more subjects is needed.

References

Bennett, S., K. Maton & L. Kervin (2008). The 'digital natives' debate: A critical review of the evidence. *British Journal of Educational Technology*, 39(5), 775–786.

Chen, G., W. Cheng, T.-W. Chang, X. Zheng & R. Huang (2014). A comparison of reading comprehension across paper, computer screens, and tablets: Does tablet familiarity matter? *Journal of Computers in Education*, 1(2–3), 213–225.

Cheong, P. (2008). The young and techless? Internet use and problem-solving behaviors among young adults in Singapore. *New Media and Society*, 10(5), 771–791.

Combes, B. (2009). Generation Y: Are they really digital natives or more like digital refugees? *Synergy*, 7(1), 31–40.

Compaine, B. M. (2001). *The Digital Divide: Facing a Crisis or Creating a Myth?*, Cambridge, MA: MIT Press.

Darnton, R. (1991). History of reading. In Peter Burke (ed.), *New Perspectives on Historical Writing*, 140–167, Cambridge: Polity.

Delgado, P., C. Vargas, R. Ackerman & L. Salmerón (2018). Don't throw away your printed books: A meta-analysis on the effects of reading media on reading comprehension. *Educational Research Review*, 25, 23–38.

Dillon, A. (1992). Reading from paper versus screens: A critical review of the empirical literature. *Ergonomics*, 35, 1297–1326.

Genette, G. (1997). *Paratexts: Thresholds of textuality of Interpretation*, Cambridge: Cambridge University Press.

Gerlach, J. & P. Buxmann (2011). *Investigating the acceptance of electronic books: The impact of haptic dissonance on innovation adoption*. European Conference on Information Systems (ECIS).

Green, M. C. & T. C. Brock (2000). The role of transportation in the persuasiveness of public narratives. *Journal of Personality and Social Psychology*, 79(5), 701–721.

Hershatter, A. & M. Epstein (2017). Millennials and the world of work: An organization and management perspective. *Journal of Business and Psychology*, 25(2), 211–223.

Helsper, E. J. & R. Enyon (2010). Digital natives: Where is the evidence? *British Educational Research Journal*, 36, 503–520.

Herring, Susan C. (2008). Questioning the generational divide: Technological exoticism and adult construction of online youth identity. In D. Buckingham (ed.), *Youth, Identity, and Digital Media*, Cambridge, MA: MIT Press, 71–92.

Howe, N. & W. Strauss (2000). *Millennials Rising: The Next Great Generation*, New York: Vintage.

Kirschner, P. A. & P. De Bruyckere 2017. The myths of the digital native and the multitasker. *Teaching and Teacher Education*, 67, 135–142.

Koschorke, A. (2016). *Adolf Hitlers "Mein Kampf": Zur Poetik des Nationalsozialismus*, Berlin: Matthes und Seitz.

Lüdtke, J., B. Meyer-Sickendieck & A. M. Jacobs (2014). Immersing in the stillness of an early morning: Testing the mood empathy hypothesis of poetry reception. *Psychology of Aesthetics, Creativity and the Arts*, 8, 363–377.

Mangen, A., & D. Kuiken (2014). Lost in the iPad: Narrative engagement on paper and tablet. *Scientific Study of Literature*, 4(2), 150–177.

Mangen, A., & A. van der Weel (2016). The evolution of reading in the age of digitization: An integrative framework for reading research. *Literacy*, 50(3), 116–124.

Mangen, A. (2016). The digitization of literary reading: Contributions from empirical research. *Orbis Litterarum*, 71(3), 240–262.

Mangen, A. (2008). Hypertext fiction reading: Haptics and immersion. *Journal of Research in Reading*, 31, 404–419.

Margolin, S. J., C. Driscoll, M. J. Toland & J. L. Kegler (2013). E-readers, computer screens, or paper: Does reading comprehension change across media platforms? *Applied Cognitive Psychology*, 27(4), 512–551.

Mayes, D. K., V. K. Sims & J. M. Koonce (2001). Comprehension and workload differences for VDT and paper-based reading. *International Journal of Industrial Ergonomics*, 28, 367–378.

Merchant, G. (2015). Keep taking the tablets: iPads, story apps

and early literacy. *Australian Journal of Language & Literacy*, 38(1), 3–11.
Noyes, J. M. & K. J. Garland (2008). Computer- vs. paper-based tasks: Are they equivalent? *Ergonomics*, 51(9), 1352–1375.
Noyes, J. M. & K. J. Garland (2003). VDT versus paper-based text: Reply to Mayes, Sims and Koonce. *International Journal of Industrial Ergonomics*, 31(6), 411–423.
Prensky, M. (2009). Listen to the natives. *Kaleidoscope: Contemporary and Classic Readings in Education*, 306–310.
Prensky, M. (2001). Digital natives, digital immigrants Part 1. *On the horizon*, 9(5), 1–6.
Johnson, M. & L. Johnson (2010). *Generations, Inc.: From Boomers to Linksters – Managing the Friction between Generations at Work*, New York: AMACOM.
Salgaro, M., P. Sorrentino, G. Lauer, J. Lüdtke & A. M. Jacobs (2018). How to measure the social prestige of a Nobel Prize in Literature? Development of a scale assessing the literary value of a text. *TXT*, 5, 138–148.
Smola, K. & C. D. Sutton (2002). Generational differences: Revisiting generational work values for the new millennium. *Journal of Organizational Behavior*, 23(4), 363–382.
Tapscott, D. (2009). *Grown Up Digital: How the Net Generation is Changing Your World*, New York: McGraw-Hill Professional.
Tapscott, D. (1997). *Growing Up Digital: The Rise of the Net Generation*. New York: McGraw-Hill.
Twenge, J. M. (2017). *iGen. The 10 Trends Shaping Today's Young People – and the Nation*, New York: Simon and Schuster.
Tyson, S. & E. Parry (2011). *Managing an Age Diverse Workforce*, Basingstoke: Palgrave Macmillan.
van der Weel, A. (2011). *Changing Our Textual Minds: Towards a Digital Order of Knowledge*, Manchester: Manchester University Press.
Wästlund, E., H. Reinikka, T. Norlader & T. Archer (2005). Effects of VDT and paper presentation on consumption and production of information: Psychological and physiological factors. *Computers in Human Behavior*, 21, 377–394.
Wolf, M. (2007). *Proust and the Squid: The Story and Science of the Reading Brain*, New York: HarperCollins.
Wolf, M. & M. Barzillai (2009). The importance of deep reading. In

M. Scherer (ed.), *Challenging the Whole Child: Reflections on Best Practices in Learning, Teaching, and Leadership*, ASCD.

Zemke, R., C. Raines & B. Filipczak (2000). *Generations at Work: Managing the Clash of Veterans, Boomers, Xers, and Nexters in Your Workplace*, New York: AMACOM.

Ziefle, M. (1998). Effects of display resolution on visual performance. *Human Factors*, 40(4), 554–568.

The object of reading

Designing a virtual reality environment for reading literature

Prelude to an experiment with *Alice's Adventures in Wonderland*

Federico Pianzola & Wayne de Fremery

This contribution presents the process of designing a virtual environment for reading using a VR headset. The aim is to set up an environment that invites readers to experience *Alice's Adventures in Wonderland* in a new way. Our VR literature concept explores the idea of books as worlds to enter. Its central questions concern how to design new media to enliven older media forms of literature. Decisions taken in the design process concern the shape given to the portions of text displayed, as well as their flow and localization in a virtual 3D space. The hypotheses to be tested in upcoming research are whether this kind of literary experience can attract new readers and help them to be more absorbed in the story – more focused and emotionally engaged – and establish a more vivid memory of what they read. This article is a description of hypotheses about how to design a VR reading environment so as to achieve these results.

Introduction

> "In another moment down went Alice after it, never once considering how in the world she was to get out again" (Carroll 1866, 3).

New media present new opportunities to design literary experiences. This article is a description of hypotheses, opportunities and challenges when designing Lewis Carroll's classic *Alice's Adventures in Wonderland* for virtual reality (VR), with the aim of enhancing readers' narrative absorption – the state of being focused on and emotionally engaged with the story (Hakemulder et al. 2017) – and readers' recall of the reading experience. Carroll's Wonderland is an apt metaphor for the choices presented when designing literary texts in virtual reality, a 'book' format that is not yet common.

The very first chapter of the novel offers prompts for a reflection on books and reading: "'and what is the use of a book,' thought Alice, 'without pictures or conversations?'" (Carroll 1866, 1–2). Moreover, the way Alice dives down the rabbit-hole resembles the way in which readers can immerse themselves in books, but it could also be a way to imagine entering a virtual 3D space in which the story unfolds. A piece of fiction in VR can be designed to elicit the feeling of falling slowly down a deep well.

Readers can be made to face the text in front of them, but they can also "look down and make out what" they are "coming to", look at the sides and see what "maps and pictures" are hung there, and wonder many other things, including whether the fall might "never come to an end" (Carroll 1866, 3–4). VR presents the opportunity to experiment with the reification of old tropes related to reading experience, such as the sense of 'getting lost in a book'.

Working with *Alice* we explore how canonical texts might be redesigned for new media formats so as to increase readers' absorption into the story and ability to recall the aesthetic experience of reading. Our desire is to make the experience of literature engrossing for as many people as possible, including those generations for whom books are not the primary source of narratives, inasmuch as they are more attracted by audiovisual and interactive stories. We want people to be readers and "never once consider how in the world" they are "to get out" of literature presented in new media, once they have gone down the "rabbit hole" we have designed for them.

Digital technologies have been exploited in different ways in relation to literature – by literary artists to create new text forms, by digital humanists for curation and criticism – but no one has yet focused on designing literary texts in VR to enhance (rather than transform) traditional reading experiences, and better understand 'traditional' literary experiences. Over the last forty years many literary works augmented by digital technology have been released, including hypertexts, multimodal novels, interactive fiction, GPS location-specific narratives, installations in immersive virtual environments and so on (Hayles 2008). Two online catalogues collect artistic projects that go under the name of 'electronic literature' or 'digital fiction' (ELO; ELMCIP), covering many examples that aim at innovating how literature is created.

Work in the Digital Humanities has often been directed toward supporting literary history and criticism, creating digital editions of literary works conceived and born in more traditional media, like printed paper or manuscripts (for example Driscoll & Pierazzo 2016). However, in addition to authors and critics, there is great potential in thinking about a third agent in the world of literature: the reader. Reading in the age of digitization can be reconceptualized, for instance by designing the reading experience for a new medium: virtual reality. In the following sections we will present the design concept for such a reading experience.

Literature in a new medium

Exploring the affordances of a new medium means experimentation aimed at identifying the core elements that constitute experiences with 'old' media – in our case, the experience of reading literature on paper and screens – in order to understand the opportunities presented by the new media.

These experiments are made by attempting to assess the role that various design elements play in an experience, which is accomplished through iteration: prototyping, testing and redesign. In many cases, this experimental process necessitates that traditional features of a media be forgone, if only temporarily, in order to understand the role that they have played traditionally, as well as the social history and technical conventions of that tradition.

For our VR Alice project, we started with the assumption, derived from cognitive narratology, that one core feature of literature is the enabling of the embodied resonance of experiences through the enactment of a story (Caracciolo 2014; Kukkonen 2020). That is, a reader's engagement with a story is prompted by the participation of their body in processes of meaning-making through the resonances evoked by motion verbs, indications of direction, bodily states, shift of perspective, rhythm, etc. With this in mind, we wished to explore how reading experiences in VR might be designed to foster the enactment of a story that will stay in readers' memories.

A second assumption is that writing systems are a primary stimulus offered by literature such as *Alice*. We have therefore focused our reflection on understanding how the conventions of writing systems might be modified for virtual environments. This focus on writing systems distinguishes our project from the growing body of work centred on interactivity and visual storytelling. Lastly, we assume that reading fiction stimulates an absorbed state and activates memory in ways that can be distinguished from other forms of media, such as films or video games (Green et al. 2008; Bálint, Kuijpers & Doicaru 2017). Starting from these assumptions, we have focused our work on attempts to understand how engagement with writing systems stimulates absorption as readers enact a story, and on the relationship between memory and this process of enacted embodiment.

Narrative absorption is an experiential state that can emerge while reading a narrative text, viewing an audiovisual narrative or using an interactive narrative artefact, such as a video game. This state is characterized by focused attention on the story world, perceived transportation into it, emotional engagement with characters and events, and vivid imagery (Green et al. 2008; Busselle & Bilandzic 2009; Kuijpers et al. 2014). Absorption and memory are intertwined inasmuch as operative memory is needed to remember anticipated and delayed information in stories (Gerrig & O'Brien 2005) – which brings about absorbing narrative effects like suspense and surprise (Sternberg 1992) – and absorbing stories are remembered longer by readers (McCabe & Peterson 1990; Cahill & McGaugh 1995).

Alice herself finds remembering stories a very useful thing to do and so she carefully checks whether the little bottle that she finds while looking for the White Rabbit is marked 'poison' or not, "for she had read several nice little stories about children who had got burnt, and eaten up by wild beasts, and other unpleasant things, all because they *would* not remember the simple rules their friends had taught them" (Carroll 1866, 10).

The stories we read add to our dictionary of experiences we

can access during sense-making processes, especially when they involve understanding natural language (cf. the concept of 'bridging inferences' in McNamara 2007). This is why it is important to make written stories more accessible and engaging for contemporary users, because narratives are a constituent of our ability to understand the world and act in it.

In the following sections we present our ideas on how to design a VR experience aimed at fostering a thought-provoking and engaging encounter with a literary masterpiece.

Designing literature for VR

In human-centred design processes a crucial aspect to keep in mind is how the *user* will interact with the system that is being designed, "focusing on the users, their needs and requirements" (ISO 2019). In our case, we are designing a virtual reality environment for reading literature and are interested in the effects of literature on people; therefore we will focus only on the affordances of VR – i.e. what the technology offers to the user (Gibson 1979) – *for readers*. We are considering how VR may be used to make reading more appealing by prompting readers to imagine the story and its characters, and to remember the "story-driven experience" (Caracciolo 2014).

A central question for us is how to use VR to increase absorption and affect memory. However, before stating our design choices, it is worth briefly mentioning two contextual factors. First, as a technology, VR does not have some inherent quality that will enhance readers' ability to recall a literary experience. As with other technologies such as print, it is how literary materials are designed that affects memory and recall. Second, the novelty of the medium is likely to affect reader experience, but initial research about reading in VR suggests novelty may only play a minor role, especially as the technology becomes more ubiquitous (Pianzola et al. 2020). With the aim of enhancing readers' absorption and ability to recall specific passages from *Alice*, in our design concept we decided to work on the affordances of VR as a medium enabling interaction with text and other visual stimuli in a 3D space. Moreover, readers can move in the 3D space thanks to the use of controllers with which they can have their virtual avatars walk, fly or teletransport. As we will see, this combination of features is relevant for both absorption and memory.

Associating words or topics with visual references is an effective technique to retain them (Carruthers 2008; Clark & Mayer 2011). Carroll himself deploys this technique in *Alice*. When the reader encounters a tail-shaped text on the page – the tale told by the Mouse (Carroll 1866, 37) – it is a surprise that makes the reader visualize something unconventional: the overlapping of a *tale* and a *tail* (see Figure 1). This is an example of how a medium can be used to support readers' enactment of the story by complementing the verbal cues given by the written text with alternative visual stimuli. In other words, the text layout enacts the semantic content and also supports a reader's enactment of the story by complementing the verbal cues of the text (Moreno & Mayer 2002; Clark & Mayer 2011). The combination of language game, text organization on the page and the visual suggestion of a shape makes the episode memorable. This is an example driven by the author's creative need, but memory devices can also be embedded in the medium independently from the story world suggested by the author.

A well-known example of the combination of text and visuals with the aim of aiding memory is a technique called 'architectural mnemonic' (also known as 'method of loci' and 'memory palace'), according to which words are associated with specific images and mentally placed in a familiar place. To remember them later, it is sufficient to imagine being in that place. This technique has been employed widely since ancient Greece and Rome, through the Middle and Modern Ages, up

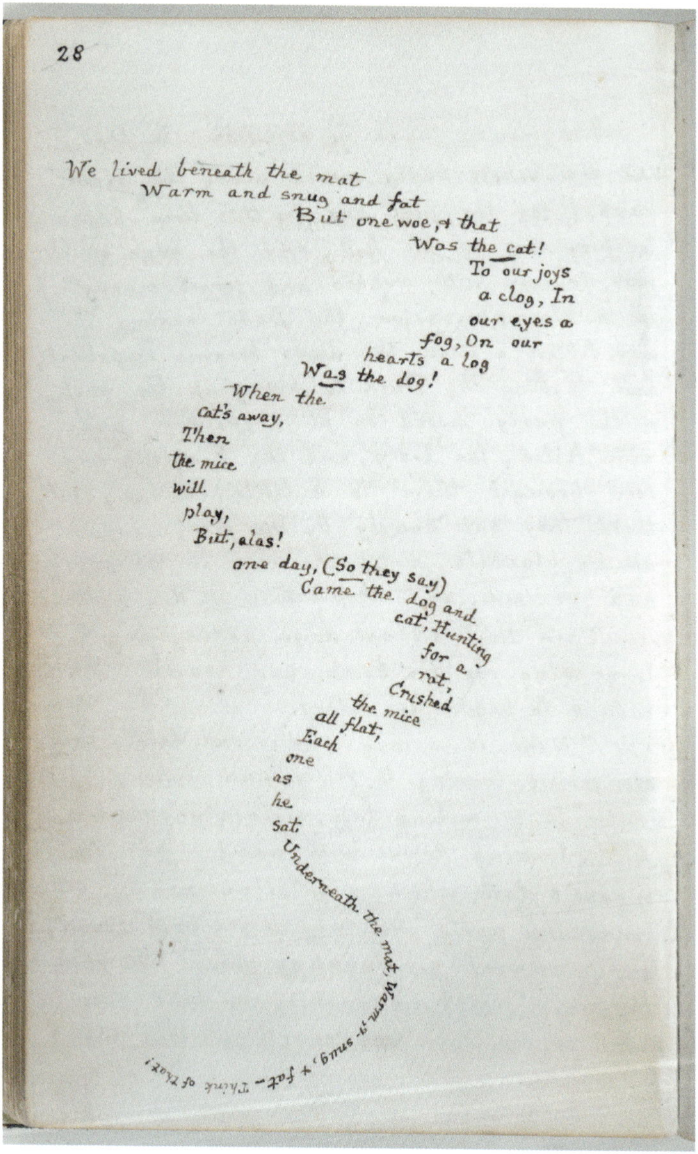

28

We lived beneath the mat
Warm and snug and fat
But one woe, & that
Was the cat!
To our joys
a clog, In
our eyes a
fog, On our
hearts a log
Was the dog!
When the
cat's away,
Then
the mice
will
play,
But, alas!
one day, (So they say)
Came the dog and
cat, Hunting
for a
rat,
Crushed
the mice
all flat,
Each
one
as
he
sat
Underneath the mat,
Warm & snug, & fat–
Think of that!

Figure 1 Page of the manuscript of Alice's Adventures Under Ground, the first book version of Alice's story (Carroll 1864)

to recent TV series (*Sherlock*), even influencing the design of manuscripts and the creation of other artefacts (Figures 2 and 3). The basic principle is that "images are retained more easily than abstract thoughts, but they 'require an abode,' for 'the embodied cannot be known without a place' ('corpus intelligi sine loco non potest')" (Carruthers 2008, 91 quoting Cicero, *De oratore*). And "'if we are not pleased with the real backgrounds available to us, we may create some in our imagination and obtain a most serviceable distribution of appropriate backgrounds' (III, 19, 32)" (Carruthers 2008, 90 quoting *Rhetorica ad Herennium*).

Architectural mnemonics, which facilitate embodied memory practices, inform our approach to the design of *Alice* for VR environments. Memory palaces are always specific to the individuals that create them. As such, it would be impossible to design a single environment that would facilitate every reader's ability to recall specific passages of *Alice* over the long term.

As many scholars have suggested, mnemonic processes rely on the activation of individual embodied agents (Dijkstra & Post 2015; Macken et al. 2016). Therefore, one way of approaching this issue is to allow readers to personalize the environment to some extent, so that they can become active users creating their own associations between text and 3D world. Another possibility is to prompt a reader's sense of being absorbed in their experience through the design of the virtual environment and the spatial organization of the text in a 3D world. Design choices affect a reader's embodied experience with the story; our task is to find design features that are likely to enable the formation of memories.

When using architectural mnemonics, readers create a mental map of the text associating each part of it with a different *locus* in space. In virtual reality we can design that mnemonic space, helping readers to recall it later thanks to the more vivid perception of embodiment that they experienced in VR (Ragan

Figure 2 Amida Gospels, Canon table, Walters Manuscript W.541, fol. 5r
Walters Art Museum. Pubic Domain

This Gospel book, with richly painted evangelist portraits, canon tables and marginal illuminations, was made in Armenia in the early 17th century. We are used to thinking of printed books mainly as texts on a white page but drawings, decorations and colour have been an important part of how knowledge has been conveyed by documents. Manuscripts in many cases provide a rich multimodal experience, involving the processing of images and text together in order to understand and remember the content of the book. The use of memory techniques was very popular among scholars and sometimes the images crafted in manuscripts were inspired by the use of these techniques. In copying the Gospels, for instance, very often an architectural space was introduced, in which the text was schematically organized between pillars. This is known as the system of Canon Tables, a concordance device invented to identify passages that appear in more than one of the four Gospels.

Figure 3 Luba. Lukasa memory board, late 19th or early 20th century

Brooklyn Museum.

The technique known as architectural mnemonics influenced the design of manuscripts but also the creation of other artefacts, like this African memory board called lukasa, a "roughly hand-sized wooden object studded with beads and pins or covered with incised or raised ideograms. During Mbudye rituals, a lukasa is used to teach neophytes sacred lore about culture heroes, clan migrations, and the introduction of sacred rule" (Roberts & Roberts 1996, 31). The marks on the board are associated with different stories that a "man of memory" enacts and perform to the community while moving his finger on the board to "visit different places". Navigating a text in a 3D virtual space may resemble this process.

2010; Krokos et al. 2019). Indeed, software enabling architectural mnemonics already exists for VR (In Formation 2018). VR space can help people visualize the architecture of textual information, visually associating it to locations in space. However, we should note that there is both positive and negative evidence about the role of contextual cues in memory processes: on one hand, contextual visual stimuli help with memory only when we are actively prompted to make associations between text and context (Humphreys & Chalmers 2016; Wälti et al. 2019), as in the case of architectural mnemonics. On the other hand, our internal states affect our ability to remember longer and more vividly (Ucros 1989). Architectural mnemonics is a very useful design concept that can lead to the design of various architectural spaces in VR – spaces that can be empirically evaluated for whether they seem to enable or disable readers' absorption and ability to recall the story-driven experience.

In the following sections we present initial designs for a VR reading experience for *Alice in Wonderland* with respect to two main aspects: the text and the 3D world in which reader and text are situated.

The text

In a semiotic sense the term 'text' should be used to refer to the whole VR artwork, but here we use it only with reference to the design of the typeset words, i.e. how the words are organized in the 3D space. In printed books the text is organized on pages which are ordered one after the other – with only one or two readable at a time – and modern readers navigate the text using page numbers, an abstract ordering system. In addition, they rely on *recto/verso* page orientations and book thickness to remember the location of a certain passage.

Conversely, e-books use position numbers and percentage to offer readers reference points. However, if the reader uses architectural mnemonics, these material features are disregarded, as she will imagine the text as located in places ('loci') that are normally not visually represented on the page – although the case of illustrated books is slightly different. In contrast to this, in VR a 3D world can be visually represented, and its spatial depth used as a reference for navigating the text. That is, if the background 3D world is a garden, we may read about the curious drink that makes Alice close up like a telescope from a paragraph located near the entrance of the garden, whereas the passage about the cake that makes her grow bigger may be located inside a pond. We will say more about the choice of the 3D background in the next section. Now we would like to focus on the disposition in space of the written words.

In terms of readers' embodied experience, VR present an opportunity to investigate questions about the materiality of printed books, such as how the linear sequences ordered in space by the stacking of pages affects memory and absorption. In principle, VR does not require the text to be linearly ordered in virtual space; different kinds of organization can be explored, also taking advantage of VR's 3D space, to bring forth the non-linear dimension of the reading experience. Strictly speaking, printed books and e-books do not enforce a linear reading – this is just one of its design affordances, one that is suggested by some cognitive and cultural schema about stories having a beginning, a middle and an end, and about our aesthetic habit of following the plot development. But reading is not only a linear process; it does not exclusively follow the unfolding of a linear sequence of events. We also sense the rhythm of the sentences, we go back and try to make sense of the words we previously read and connect different elements, refiguring what we learned (Ricoeur 1984). The non-linearity of reading is what allows the emergence of a story-driven experience, a process in which enaction and memory are strongly elicited (Caracciolo 2014). And since we want to prompt the interplay of embodiment and memory precisely to make the story-driven experience more engrossing, working on the non-linear patterns of reading is likely to be an appropriate strategy when designing a VR reading solution.

Placing the words in a 3D space enables forms of textual organization that can be very different from the typeset pages of printed books. It is also different from the interface of e-books read on smartphones and tablets, which enables one to see only small parts of text at a time. Reading on screen, however, allows a fluid typesetting that can be personalized by the reader, changing font and size, and even choosing between tapping and scrolling to see the next chunk of text. In VR, we can have an even more fluid typesetting, with the whole text distributed in space and present at all times, not just accessible through the framing of pages stacked one after the other. This affordance of VR can also aid memory. Seeing the whole text distributed in space enables a reader to associate passages with specific locations.

In a manner of speaking, the text distributed in three-dimensional space can be an opportunity to build the story articulated by the text and locations for particular memories. The ability to map text to more individually distinct locations using VR technologies promises to help readers make connections between different parts of the text, thereby activating inferential processes about story development (Gerrig & O'Brien 2005; Kukkonen 2019). It is also likely to help readers remember passages of the story, since the associations of text and places can trigger suspenseful absorption (Kuzmičová 2016). For instance, a reader at the entrance of the garden can anticipate with a quick look what is in the text, seeing that on her path she will encounter a "Pool of tears", a "Mad tea-party" and the "Queen's croquet-ground". Looking at the pond in the distance she may wonder what will happen when she reaches the text located in that place, and why the text she has in front of her is near a bush, but the text that she will eventually come to read is floating on water. How this affects the reading process and narrative effects more broadly will have to be determined with empirical testing. However, our choice is supported by evidence that maps are an effective tool for the purpose of remembering (Allen 2004) and that there is neurological relation between spatial navigation and episodic memory (Burgess et al. 2002; Solomon et al. 2019).

By emphasizing 3D space as a design element that can aid readers' recall of their experience with *Alice* in VR, we do not want to displace the linearity needed by the plot development altogether; our aim is rather to valorise non-linear reading patterns because they are crucial for the embodied engagement involved in absorbed reading and mnemonic processes. For this reason, we propose a design solution that involves arranging blocks of text grouped in various locations of the 3D space (Figure 4). In this way it is possible to implement both a linear and a non-linear pattern at the same time: blocks of text that follow each other in the story are arranged in contiguous zones of the 3D space.

The reader will access the VR edition entering the 3D space from a point of view that allows them to see the text distributed in the world all around herself. This choice allows the reader to look at the overall 'architecture' of text and world – getting a sense of their current location in the textual space – and encourages them to remember the blocks of text not just as coming one after the other but also as associated with various locations of the environment. Thus, mnemonic processes can be activated both by the progression of the story (such as emotionally intense events, which are more memorable) and by their relationship with elements of the environment. We hypothesise that readers seeing themselves situated inside a world with a text will mean that they are more likely to activate embodied cognitive and affective responses – a sense of

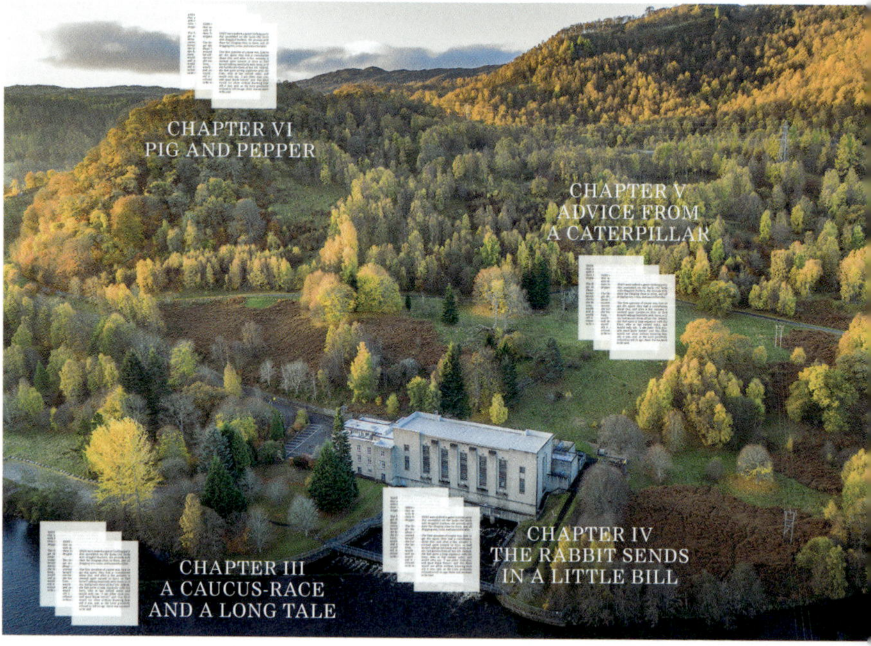

Figure 4. Image representing the reader's initial position when accessing the VR edition of the story

Original photo by Ian Dick. Creative Commons-BY

The paragraphs are arranged in blocks of text located in the 3D world so that the reader is able to see the whole book organized around her. Some parts of the book are not visible in this figure because they are located outside the reader's field of view. This text distribution allows the reader to follow the linear progression of the story one paragraph after the other, as a journey from the lake to the top of the hill, but it also enables non-linear exploration, since it is possible to see the whole text and move to a specific location at will.

presence (Lombard et al. 2015) – that will help to create more intense absorption and consequently stronger memories of the reading experience (cf. Krokos et al. 2019).

Since in VR typesetting is no longer bounded by the material structure of the book, the page no longer needs to be the organisational unit of the text: a smaller unit – the paragraph, for instance – will probably be a better fit for the VR medium. There are two main reasons supporting this choice. First, smaller text units are nowadays more familiar for many people, since they are the most common format on social media; thus, having a less intimidating text extension may be more user-friendly for occasional readers (cf. Baron 2015). A second more technical reason concerns VR headsets. Their lenses are curved and, consequently, only small segments of text displayed in the centre of the field of view remain in focus. To see the text placed outside the focus point clearly, the reader has to move her head (not just her eyes), so that the required part will be seen through the centre of the lens. Accordingly, the best solution seems to be displaying a portion of text on a surface of limited extension, placing it at the appropriate distance to be seen in focus without discomfort (Kreylos 2016).

Reading in VR will require head movements and gestures that are different from those we commonly make when reading printed books. When seated the reader will be able to read the block of texts in front of her, moving between paragraphs by swiping with a hand controller. Then she can virtually move to the block of text located in a different zone of the 3D space by pointing at it with the controller. This is not too different from reading a text on a computer monitor or scrolling through a novel on a smartphone. The evolution of the materiality of and our interaction with books is part of our cultural history: in the past, reading scrolls gave way to turning the pages of a printed book.

The 3D world

We designed text distribution in a 3D space with the aim of fostering memory. The 3D world in which the text is placed contributes to such functions as well, but it is also designed to sustain the activation of absorbed reading by providing visual stimuli.

With respect to memory, we presented the process of mental enrichment elicited by the text distribution in space. However, in our concept readers can also add objects and signs of their choice to the 3D world, to make the background more familiar to them, just as they would annotate on paper or use different coloured post-its to bookmark interesting parts of a book. Giving readers the chance to personalize the 3D world is a way of enabling active reading, but another issue has to be also considered, namely deciding what kind of background should be provided in order to further prompt absorption and memory.

In her exploration of the possible benefits of VR for narrative, Marie-Laure Ryan assumes that the 3D world should represent the narrative world, thus concluding that "stories in which landscape and setting feature prominently ... benefit from the ... increase in spatial immersion" (Ryan 2015, 255). We disagree and think that the 3D world should not represent the story world, because this would provide visual elements that have a strong impact on the reader's attention, making them less engaged with the verbal component of the story (Green et al. 2008). On the other hand, making it completely unrelated to the story does not seem a fruitful option either. Preliminary tests with readers revealed that they enjoyed some kind of connection between the background and the story (Pianzola et al. 2019). Therefore, we propose using a 3D background that has some relevant connection with the text.

For *Alice*, a garden may be a good option, since there is a thematic affinity with the story setting. For other kinds of stories, with scenes in very different geographical places or more focused on the psychological processes of the characters, the challenge is to find a suitable 3D world that can valorise the thematic, stylistic and narrative features of the literary work. For instance, for Primo Levi's *The Truce* – recounting a long journey from Auschwitz to Turin through post-World War II Europe – we could choose to use either a map on which the reader can follow the character's movements, like the one Levi himself had at the beginning of his book, or a more abstract background with different isolated places floating like islands in a dark void. In general, the duty to create an appropriate 3D world in which to place the text will be part of the creative and editorial process of VR literature.

Beside designing the 3D world for increasing readers' absorption, if we are also going to consider the role of embodiment for remembering, in the *Rhetorica ad Herennium* there are some suggestions for how to pick an appropriate background when building an architectural mnemonic. These are suggestions that can be also tested in VR:

> Background *loci* should be well lighted but not glaring; they must not be too much alike but differ enough in form to be clearly distinguishable one from the next; they should be of moderate size and extent, "for when excessively large they render the images vague, and when too small often seem incapable of receiving an arrangement of images" ... These backgrounds should be viewed from about thirty feet [nine meters] away, "for, like the external eye, so the inner eye of thought is less powerful when you have moved the object of sight too near or too far away" (III, 19, 32). (Carruthers 2008, 90)

This may be a valuable suggestion for memorizing in general, but we are here concerned with memory in relation to the aesthetic experience of reading literature. In the design process, when making choices concerning the position of the reader in the 3D world, we have to consider their effect on both absorption and memory. One issue to be addressed is whether the distance between the background and the reader's point of view should be the one suggested by the ancient masters of rhetoric, or whether the evolution of narrative forms should be made manifest, thus allowing the reader's point of view in virtual reality to follow the perspective of the characters. The sensorimotor enactment prompted by the way the story is told is very important for narrative absorption: for instance, action verbs and textual cues about characters' perception are more effective than impersonal narration (Speer et al. 2009).

Consider the case of a third-person narrator commenting on the story events (cf. Hühn et al. 2013): "[Alice was saying] 'I shall have to ask them what the name of the country is, you know. Please, Ma'am, is this New Zealand or Australia?' (and she tried to curtsey as she spoke – fancy *curtseying* as you're falling through the air! Do you think you could manage it?)" (Carroll 1866, 5). The background matched with this passage should take into account the style and narrative effects of the text, because they contribute significantly to the story-driven experience that we want readers to remember.

Since the humorous effect relies on the ideological distance between the character and the reader – who is led to acknowledge that Alice is being portrayed as a very playful and unique girl – it may be odd to have a background seen from a short distance, bringing the reader too close to what might be the character's perspective. Hence, in this case, the nine metre's distance suggested in the *Rhetorica ad Herennium* may be a good option, since it reflects the detachment needed to appreciate the narrator's humour. But consider when the same narrator shifts to the character's focalization: "Alice was not a bit hurt, and she jumped up on to her feet in a moment: she looked up, but it was all dark overhead; before her was another long passage, and the White Rabbit was still in sight, hurrying down it. There was not a moment to be lost: away went Alice like the wind" (Carroll 1866, 7). In this scene the narrator focuses on Alice's self-perception of her own body and adopts her perspective to describe the narrative space around her. Likewise, the sentence "There was not a moment to be lost" is a cue strongly attached to Alice's perspective; it is not just a represented thought – it is unlikely someone would explicitly think this – rather it is the verbalization of the character's perception of urgency and her concurrent bodily activation. In this case, a background seen from a nine-metre distance is not very appropriate, since it may counteract the focalization effect triggered by textual cues.

Having considered the implications of two very different examples, our concept for the virtual 3D space focuses on assessing how VR can help intensify readers' absorption and enhance their ability to recall literary language and the experience elicited by it. The idea that the background should be seen from a distance matching the perspective given by narrative voice and focalization comes from the need not to create cognitive dissonance between the enactment suggested by the words and the physical location of the reader in the 3D world.

It is significant for the activation of absorption to have a variable perspectival distance, so that readers can be prompted to follow the modulation of narrative focalization, sometimes seeing the background from afar and sometimes enacting the character's point of view. This could be achieved by placing the various blocks of text at different distances from the 3D background, based on the main focalization employed in each block of text (Figure 5). This architectural choice enables the reader to see the background world with an aerial perspective (the nine metres suggested by the ancient rhetoricians) when reading some parts of the story. In other cases, she will be able to see the 3D world more closely, alongside the part of text she is reading.

This solution allows the deployment of the architectural mnemonic technique with a variable perspectival distance from the background.

Conclusion

With the hope of making the experience of reading literature more engrossing for 21st century readers, we have proposed some initial design concepts to be tested in future empirical research. Our choices have been guided by a desire to enhance the embodiment of readers interacting with texts so that the story-driven experience will be better remembered. They have also been guided by a desire to take advantage of the affordances provided by VR to engender more memorable textual experiences. Architectural mnemonics influenced our decisions conceptually and lead to the following choices:

- display paragraphs as basic text unit
- organise paragraphs in blocks of text that are situated in different locations of the 3D world
- place the reader's initial point of view in a position allowing them to see the entirety of the 3D world and the blocks of text distributed in it
- choose a 3D background world not mimetically representing the story setting but having a thematic affinity to it
- place the blocks of text closer to or farther from the background world, according to narrative focalization

We made these choices in order to shape *Alice* into a literary experience in virtual reality that enhances the imaginative and mnemonic experience of those that encounter Carroll's story in virtual space. We hope that our description of how we came to make these choices might be useful to broader discussions

Figure 5 Two frames representing the variable reader's point of view

Original photos by stillwellmike and Tristan Ferris. Creative Commons-BY

On top, the default position, with the background seen from afar. On the bottom, the position for those paragraphs in which the narrator adopts character's focalization. The movements of the reader's point of view in VR aim at visually supporting the story enactment elicited by verbal cues focused on the character's perception. To avoid distortions, the distance between the reader and the text will be always the same, so that for the reader there is no perceived change in text size.

about methods for reiterating literary classics in virtual reality and other emerging media, taking advantage of the affordances of technology.

We chose to focus on two very specific aspects – narrative absorption and memory – which do not exemplify the variety of effects that literature can achieve. We provided arguments supporting our decisions and explained the motivations behind the design process. However, we are aware that this is just one of the possibilities offered by VR. In the future, we will proceed in this direction but we will also experiment with alternative solutions to find the best design to boost the power of reading in the era of digital technology.

References

Allen, G. L. (ed.) (2004). *Human Spatial Memory: Remembering Where*, Mahwah: Lawrence Erlbaum Associates.

Amida Gospels. 17th Century. Walters Art Museum. Accessed 7 January 2019. thedigitalwalters.org/Data/WaltersManuscripts/W541/data/W.541/sap/W541_000011_sap.jpg.

Baron, N. S. (2015). *Words Onscreen: The Fate of Reading in a Digital World*, New York: Oxford University Press.

Burgess, N., E. A. Maguire & J. O'Keefe (2002). The human hippocampus and spatial and episodic memory. *Neuron*, 35(4), 625–641.

Busselle, R. & H. Bilandzic (2009). Measuring narrative engagement. *Media Psychology* 12(4), 321–347.

Cahill, L. & J. L. McGaugh (1995). A novel demonstration of enhanced memory associated with emotional arousal. *Consciousness and Cognition* 4(4), 410–421.

Caracciolo, M. (2014). *The Experientiality of Narrative: An Enactivist Approach*, Berlin: de Gruyter.

Carroll, L. (1864). *Alice's Adventures Under Ground*, Manuscript. Oxford. bl.uk/manuscripts/FullDisplay.aspx?ref=Add_MS_46700. Accessed 7 January 2019.

Carroll, L. (1866). *Alice's Adventures in Wonderland*, New York: Appleton.

Carroll, L. (1872). *Through the Looking Glass: And What Alice Found There*, London: Macmillan.

Carruthers, M. (2008). *The Book of Memory: A Study of Memory in Medieval Culture*, Cambridge: Cambridge University Press.

Clark, R. C. & R. E. Mayer (2011). *E-learning and the Science of Instruction: Proven Guidelines for Consumers and Designers of Multimedia Learning*, San Francisco: Pfeiffer.

Dijkstra, K. & L. Post (2015). Mechanisms of embodiment. *Frontiers in Psychology*, 6: 1525.

ELMCIP (2019). *Electronic literature knowledge base*. Accessed 7 January 2019. elmcip.net/knowledgebase.

ELO (2019). *Electronic literature directory*. Accessed 7 January 2019. directory.eliterature.org.

Gerrig, R. J. & E. J. O'Brien (2005). The scope of memory-based processing. *Discourse Processes*, 39(2–3), 225–242.

Gibson, J. J. (1979). *The Ecological Approach to Visual Perception*, Boston: Houghton Mifflin Harcourt.

Green, M. C., S. Kass, J. Carrey, B. Herzig, R. Feeney & J. Sabini (2008). Transportation across media: Repeated exposure to print and film. *Media Psychology*, 11(4), 512–539.

Hakemulder, F., M. M. Kuijpers, E. S. Tan, K. Bálint & M. M. Doicaru (eds.) (2017). *Narrative Absorption*, Amsterdam: John Benjamins.

Hayles, K. (2008). *Electronic Literature: New Horizons for the Literary*, Notre Dame, IN: University of Notre Dame Press.

Hühn, P., J. C. Meister, J. Pier & W. Schmid (eds.) (2013). *The Living Handbook of Narratology*, Hamburg: Hamburg University Press. Accessed 7 January 2019. lhn.uni-hamburg.de.

In Formation, Inc. (2018). *Loci memory palace*. Accessed 7 January 2019. iform.us/ssite/2018/07/13/loci-memory-palace.

ISO (2019). *Ergonomics of human-system interaction – Part 210: human-centred design for interactive systems (ISO 9241-210:2019)*. Accessed 22 November 2019. iso.org/standard/77520.html.

Kreylos, O. (2016). *Head-mounted displays and lenses*. Accessed 7 January 2019. doc-ok.org/?p=1360.

Krokos, E., C. Plaisant & A. Varshney (2019). Virtual memory palaces: Immersion aids recall. *Virtual Reality*, 23(1), 1–15.

Kuijpers, M. M., F. Hakemulder, E. S. Tan & M. M. Doicaru (2014). Exploring absorbing reading experiences: developing and validating a self-report scale to measure story world absorption. *Scientific Study of Literature*, 4(1), 89–122.

Kukkonen, K. 2020. *Probability Designs: Literature and Predictive Processing*, Oxford: Oxford University Press.

Kuzmičová, A. (2016). Does it matter where you read? Situating narrative in physical environment. *Communication Theory*, 26(3), 290–308.

Lombard, M., F. Biocca, J. Freeman, W. Ijsselsteijn & R. J. Schaevitz (eds.) (2015). *Immersed in Media: Telepresence Theory, Measurement & Technology*, Cham: Springer.

Macken, B., J. C. Taylor, M. D. Kozlov, R. W. Hughes & D. M. Jones (2016). Memory as embodiment: The case of modality and serial short-term memory. *Cognition*, 155, 113–124.

McCabe, A. & C. Peterson (1990). What makes a narrative memorable? *Applied Psycholinguistics*, 11(1), 73–82.

McNamara, D. S. (ed.) (2007). *Reading Comprehension Strategies: Theories, Interventions, and Technologies*, New York: Lawrence Erlbaum Associates.

Moreno, R. & R. E. Mayer (2002). Learning science in virtual reality multimedia environments: role of methods and media. *Journal of Educational Psychology* 94(3), 598–610.

Pianzola, F., J. Weller & K. Balint (2019). Virtual reality as a tool for promoting reading via enhanced narrative absorption and empathy. *Scientific Study of Literature*, 9(2), 162–193.

Ragan, E. D. (2010). The effects of higher levels of immersion on procedure memorization performance and implications for educational virtual environments. *Presence: Teleoperators and Virtual Environments*, 19(6), 527–543.

Ricoeur, P. (1984). *Time and Narrative*, Chicago: University of Chicago Press.

Roberts, M. N. & A. F. Roberts (1996). Luba art and the making of history. *African Arts*, 29(1), 22–35.

Ryan, M.-L. (2015). *Narrative as Virtual Reality 2: Revisiting Immersion and Interactivity in Literature and Electronic Media*, Baltimore: Johns Hopkins University Press.

Sherlock (2007–2010). TV series. Created by Mark Gatiss and Steven Moffat. BBC.

Solomon, E. A., B. C. Lega, M. R. Sperling & M. J. Kahana (2019). Hippocampal theta codes for distances in semantic and temporal spaces. *Proceedings of the National Academy of Sciences*, November. doi.org/10.1073/pnas.1906729116.
Speer, N. K., J. R. Reynolds, K. M. Swallow & J. M. Zacks (2009). Reading stories activates neural representations of visual and motor experiences. *Psychological Science*, 20(8), 989–999.
Sternberg, M. (1992). Telling in time (II): Chronology, teleology, narrativity. *Poetics Today*, 13(3), 463–541.

A canvas for studying the processes and effects used in artists' books

A visual essay

Chloé Aubry & Claire Gauzente

This visual essay proposes a framework for studying the different plastic processes used in artists' books and their potential impact on the reader/book activator. The tripartite view of human mind (cognition, conation, emotion) is our underlying guide (Hilgard 1980, Pratkanis et al. 2014).

The empirical basis is a corpus of 80 artists' books analysed in terms of plastic processes (Aubry, 2014). Thirty different types of interventions have been identified and grouped into four main higher-level categories: (1) interventions in the formal external aspect (**EXT**); (2) interventions in internal architecture and organization (**ARCHI**); (3) plastic interventions on pages (**PLAST**); and (4) choices of raw materials (**MAT**).

Adapted from Robert Filliou

To conduct this research, we built a corpus of 11 contemporary artists' books.

Binet, J. (2017). *Le mauvais pli*, Paris: Ed. du Rouergue.

Boom, I. & M. Lommen (2013). *Irma Boom: The Architecture of the Book*, translated by John A. Lane, Amsterdam: University of Amsterdam Bijzondere collecties.

D. Bretesche et al. (2007). *Promesse de pluie*, Nantes: autoedition

De Beir, D. & C. Pennequin (2010). *Trou Types (études de caracteres)*, Friville-Escarbotin: Friville Editions.

Filliou, R. (1998). *Toi, par lui et moi*. Bruxelles/ Crisnée: Lebeer Hossmann/Yellow Now.

Loomis, F. J. C. (2009). *Peut-être*, Rennes: Ed. Lorem Ipsum.

Millard, F. (2015). *Basic Space*, Bordeaux: EXTRA.

Munari, B. (2009). *Libro illeggibile MN 1*, 7th ed., Mantova: Corraini Editore.

Nedelec, J. (2008). *Feuilleté*, Brest: Editions Zédélé.

s.d. *Peau de phoque*, Nantes: Kraft Kollection.

Villers, B. (2015). *Left Right*, Saint-Senoux/Bruxelles/Chicago: Incertain Sens/Le Nouveau Remorqueur/Journal of Artists' Books.

Dimension 1: Proximity to codex

The 'proximity to codex' axis is not restricted to binding style, but indicates closeness to the ordinary, canonical book form more generally, in terms of size, materials and so on.

The 11 books in our sub-corpus are classified along the 'proximity to codex' axis with an indication of the main plastic processes they exemplify.

Codex proximity (—)

Basic Space
ARCHI: binding (foldable book),
EXT: book's orientation

Left Right
ARCHI: binding (flaps)

Peau de phoque
ARCHI: binding (concertina),
PLAST: cutouts

Promesse de pluie
ARCHI: binding (concertina)
EXT: page orientation

Libro illeggibile MN 1
PLAST: cutouts

Irma Boom: The Architecture of the Book
EXT: format

Trou Types (études de caractères)
PLAST: holes pierced through the page

Peut-être
ARCHI: binding (single fold)

Feuilleté
ARCHI: sequence of pages

Le mauvais pli
ARCHI: fold in the double page

Toi, par lui et moi
PLAST: pages left blank, to be completed (drawing and writing)

Codex proximity (+)

Dimension 2: Interactivity

This axis corresponds to the degree to which the reader's involvement is solicited. Such involvement may be manual or intellectual (where the understanding of something leads to a specific manual action), or emotional (where humour guides manual actions).

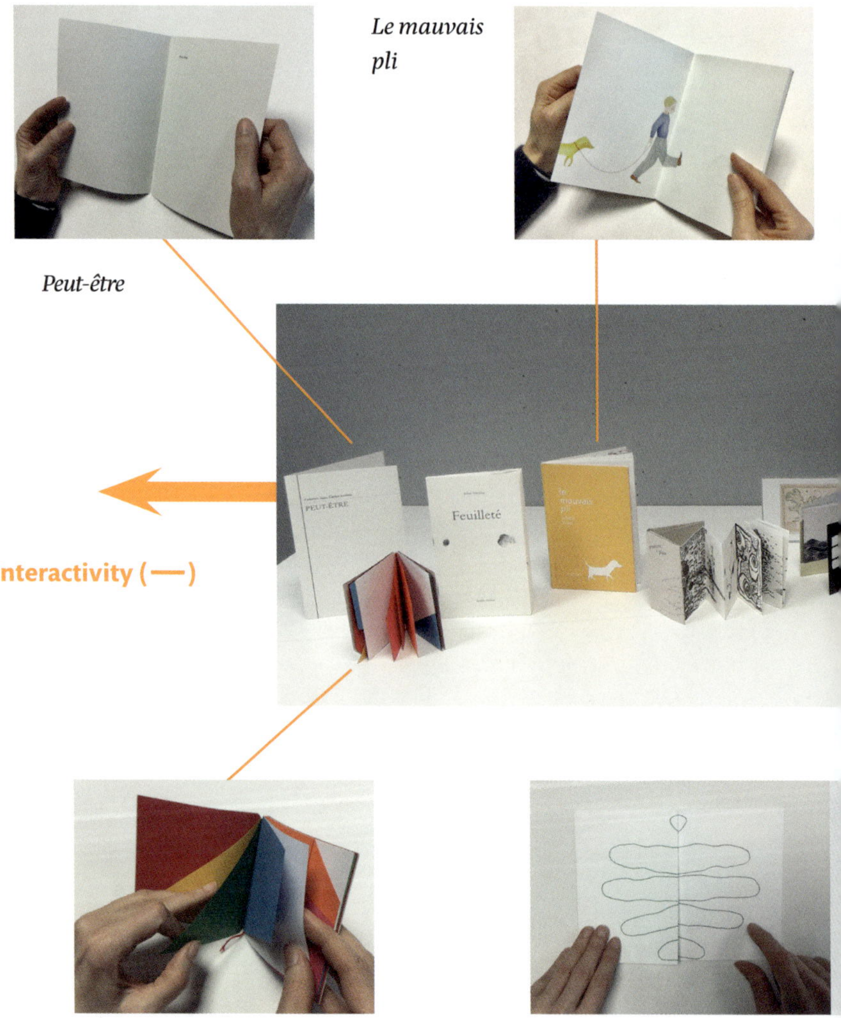

Libro illeggibile MN 1

Left Right

Trou Types (études de caractères)

Interactivity (+)

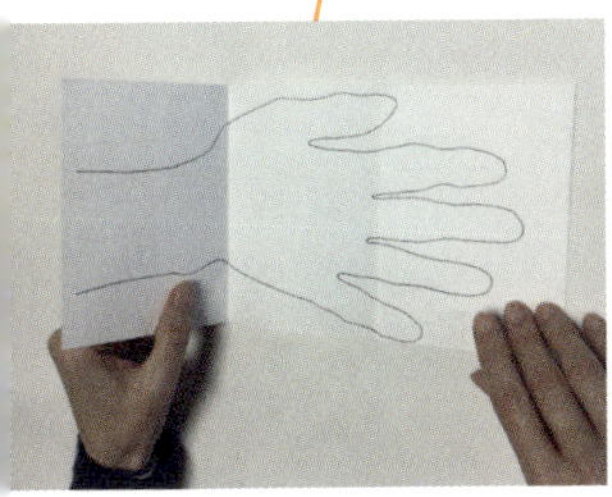

Toi, par lui et moi

Proposed canvas for studying process and effects of artists' books

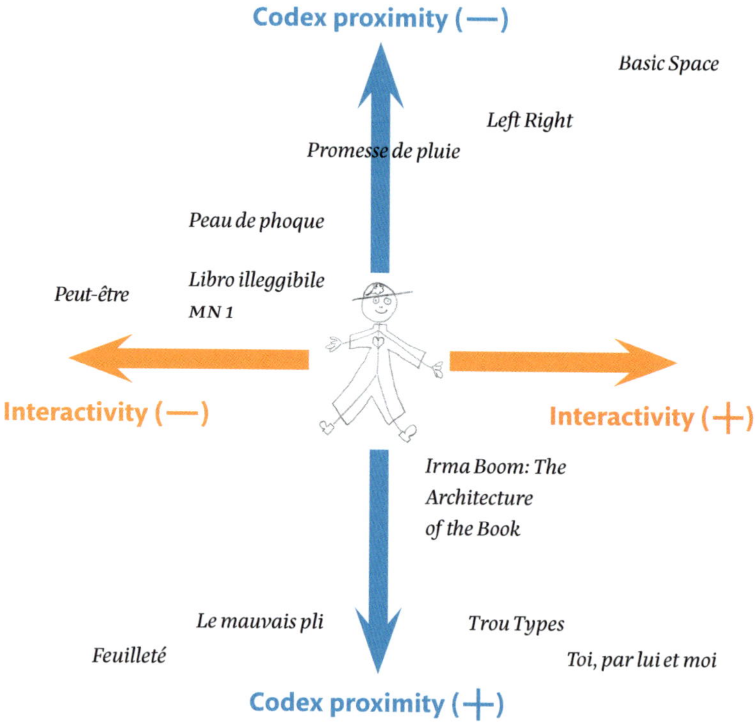

Contributions:

- empirically based on an extensive corpus of artists' books
- first step toward a rigorous study of artists' books' processes and their impact on reader
- robust (non-tautological) framework tested on a subsample of books

Research limitations of the framework:

- demonstration based on a sub-sample of books
- omits characteristics of readers
- focused on first encounters with the books

Future research avenues:

- incorporating reader's characteristics
- incorporating contextual and environmental features
- examining temporal dynamics or emotional (where humour guides manual actions).

References

Aubry, C. (2014). *Comment la matérialité du livre participe-t-elle à la narration dans l'album de jeunesse?* Master's thesis, Université du Mans.

Bodman, S. & T. Sowden (2010). *A Manifesto for the Book*, Impact Press: Bristol.

Brogowski, L. (2016). *Éditer l'art: le livre d'artiste et l'histoire du livre*, rev. ed., Rennes: Éditions Incertain Sens.

Drucker, J. (1994–2004). *The Century of Artists' Books*, Granary Books: New York.

Drucker, J. (1997). The self-conscious codex: Artists' books and electronic media. *SubStance*, 26(1).

Gauzente, C. (2018). A cluster account of the artist's book concept – Paving the way to non-essentialist thinking. *Book Arts Newsletter*, 116, 62–64. www.bookarts.uwe.ac.uk/pdf/newspdfs/116.pdf.

Hilgard, E. R. (1980). The trilogy of mind: Cognition, affection, and conation. *Journal of the History of the Behavioral Sciences*, 16(2), 107–117.

Moeglin-Delcroix, A. & Bibliothèque nationale de France (1997). *Esthétique du livre d'artiste: 1960–1980*, Paris: J.-M. Place.

Pratkanis, A. R., S. J. Breckler & A. G. Greenwald (2014). *Attitude structure and function*, Psychology Press.

Engaging with the text

Folksonomy and metadata

How the way we access information has changed

Valeria Levratto

In this article we discuss how the concept of 'index' changes when it transforms and evolves into tagging. In this transformation, the concept of 'social' determines a basic principle of indexation where each user, and not only experts, can collaborate in perfect harmony with the philosophy of web 2.0. In this digital scenario, texts have been transformed into databases: in the web 2.0 indexing process, search engines (Google, Yahoo, etc.) convey our access to information and every text must be aligned with this new format. Metadata that are invisible to users offers information to search engines, represented on a page as content and thus becoming a determining element for the distribution of knowledge and information.

The guide for the website: the folksonomy

For a long time, the index has been the tool used to organize information alphabetically and visualize content, creating a hierarchical space of names, ideas and concepts. A structure of linear thinking is thus reproduced to provide a formed and fixed order thanks to the sequentiality of a summary, as well as the division and numbering of paragraphs. In this context, Weinberger (2005, 3) says: "We have spent an inordinate amount of time encouraging experts and authorities to construct huge structures of classification, from trees of life to trees of knowledge".

In the digital era the concept of indexing has been revolutionized. It has become a 'folksonomy', a term coined by Thomas Vander Wal (2007) to denote a system where the participation of individuals is basic in the process of categorizing information, the result of personal free tagging of information and objects (anything with a URL) for one's own retrieval.

It is likely that the only important similarity between an index and a folksonomy is "the capacity for organization and representation of knowledge that both have" (Monreal & Gil 2010, 379), while an important difference is that: "while thesauri pursue of ambiguous terminology through the standardization and control of vocabulary to achieve better storage and retrieval of information, in folksonomies, on the other hand, users employ their own natural language". In addition, it is important to emphasize that tagging (in a folksonomy) has a personal dimension in which the user creates their tag index and then accesses it, while the index is created unilaterally by the author or editor of the text, who has also created different sections (chapters, paragraphs, etc.) of the text, for all readers.

Tagging is a shared and distributed action where objects and resources are described through tags, known as 'keywords', that refer us to a site and at the same time the personal annotation of content that we share with all users of the web. On some platforms, users can also vote on tags that have already been added, contributing an additional social aspect to make social tags. Some of the most popular pages that use folksonomies are Flickr, Tumblr, Blogspot and Blogger.

Tagging, as a phenomenon, contains the existing medium of classification (replaceable with annotation, categorization, etc.), but is extended to far greater ratios of massification, which makes it a new medium entirely (Monnin et al. 2009).

This new mode of classification is a purely collaborative action which is characterized by a non-linear organization of information, involving consideration of how the user perceives the term employed in the tag, and receiving the indistinct contribution of all participants. It is a very spontaneous classification since users classify information according to criteria in the moment.

The collaborative nature of this directory has meant this phenomenon, in most cases, is called 'social tagging'. Social tagging is usually defined in opposition to standardised hierarchical indexing, as it is "the process by which many users add metadata in the form of keywords to shared content" (Golder & Huberman 2006, 198). It is used for applications that encourage users to share their descriptions (or tags) of resources openly with other users, so other people with similar interests can view the links through categories or tags, or randomly. This new form of directory is particularly relevant if we consider that the use and order of tags is what determines movements and navigation between one page and another within the myriad of online cultural products. The meta-index of web 2.0 is now the result of the thoughts and conceptions of words by millions of people, visible in web 3.0.

Currently, there are many disciplines that are studying the phenomenon of folksonomies as a digital practice that many people perform daily. Hedden (2010, 238) writes: "tagging involves any kind of designation about a piece of content, what it is or what it is about ... it can include content type, date, creator, source, audience, location, rights, keywords, etc.... Tagging is a sort of the modern word for cataloging or the assignment of metadata". There are many concerns regarding the exclusivity and homogeneity that this new type of index can create. As Weinberger (2005, 3) explains: "Some have complained that a folksonomy can become a tyranny of the majority, favoring one language or one set of concepts over another". However, this author emphasises the importance that folksonomies have as a form of mental work similar to that of the human brain. Additionally, the simplicity of use that characterizes folksonomy, since the creation of terms is very easy, represents an advantage of this system, where every user has the ability to make labels.

In general, although the folksonomy is defined as "a flat space of keywords" (Quintarelli et al. 2005) because tags do not have a hierarchical structure, it is significant that this classification system is vital for some pages, like Flickr, where files can contain millions of images and where a classification at the central level would be very onerous. In Table 1 we can appreciate some advantages and disadvantages of the folksonomy.

It is very important to consider the value that each classification system may have; often a combination of both is preferable, depending on the classification and cataloguing to be performed.

Tags as metadata

In the field of computer science, the term 'tag' is widely used to describe metadata. Before the arrival of the digital age, our metadata were library cards, and books were our data. Currently 'metadata' means data that describe other data: a small quantity of very structured data that represents the contents of the data quality, data structure, information and other attributes. Metadata are useful tags important for both research and the classifications process, as well as for physically and logistically locating a document. An excellent management of metadata facilitates the analysis of the path of data from the source, and making the auto-documentation, as well as the transformation, analysis and reporting functions. Thanks to the descriptive

Table 1 Advantages and disadvantages of the folksonomy

Advantages	*Disadvantages*
Reflects trends	It has a (biased) tendency, and its is subjective
Monitors change and popularity	More appropriate for finding out information (discoverability) than research aimed (findability)
Is cheaper and quicker (than a taxonomy)	Doesn't scale well a large volume of file (inaccurate)
Facilitates workplace democracy	A large number of tags can be very indefinite and imprecise, which can difficult research
Facilitates the distribution of management tasks	There's no reference structure that connects social tags
Responds to users need	Many labels and acronyms are used
Is flexible: orders files (by date, alphabetic order, by topic, etc)	The visual size may induce to use a tag match to describe the contents instead of other more appropriate features

metadata and structure in place, information architects and interface designers can experiment with hundreds of ways of presenting navigation options. The interface can be tested and refined over time, while the faceted classification provides an enduring foundation (Rosenfeld et al. 2015, 224).

According to Gayatri and Ramachandran (2007), metadata are also used for searching – metadata must provide sufficient information to allow a user to discover whether there is data of interest within the collection of available data, and allow for its recovery: the metadata must provide sufficient information that users may acquire the data that is of interest. In this sense, it is analogous to the procedure one follows in a library to find a book.

Figure 1 is a visualisation of the interface of the website Calibre, a popular e-book manager where users can organize the metadata of all their archived books through different tags, which they can also annotate with comments.

To give further detail, we can say that metadata can be the header of a multimedia file (image, video or audio); the summary of a document; the words extracted from a text; the chips of catalogues in any format (ISBD, MARC, etc.); IP addresses or DNS; indexes of documents on an intranet; and terms extracted by indexing/search engines. In Table 2 we can appreciate some diverse types of metadata – descriptive, structural and administrative – according to the function they have in organising the information.

Table 2 Three different types of metadata

Descriptive metadata	Their task is to describe a resource with the aim of identifying it in a more in-depth way
Structural metadata	They perform the task of describing the structural composition of the file to which they are associated, as a book index
Administrative metadata	They inform about data such as: file type, author and creation date

Although 'metadata' is arguably a less familiar term among creators and consumers of networked digital content who are not information professionals, those same individuals are "increasingly adept at creating, exploiting, and assessing user-contributed metadata such as title, description, and key word tags for web pages; terms from so-called folksonomies; and social bookmarks" (Gilliland 2016, 15).

For that reason, it has become very necessary that not only professionals, but also other creators and users of digital content "understand the critical roles and potential uses of

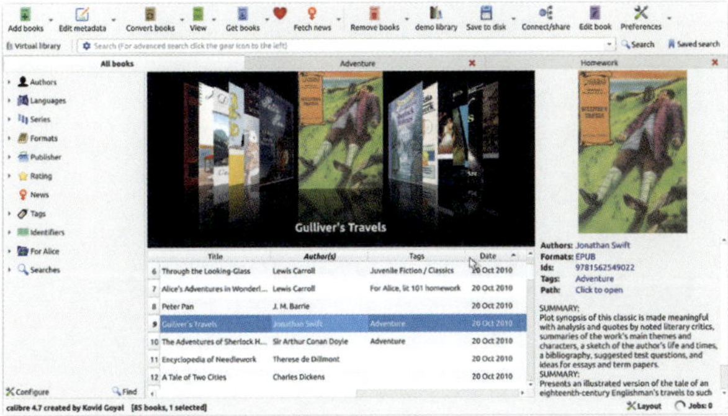

Figure 1 Calibre website, where e-book metadata can be edited by users

different types of metadata in ensuring accessible, authoritative, interoperable, scalable, and preservable cultural heritage information and record-keeping systems" (Gilliland 2016, 3).

Individuals, communities and institutions have created shared metadata standards that organise their content. It is important to remember that these legacy or previous systems may still only serve specialised knowledge communities: "Each community maintains its own structure and rules for fields of access, description, and vocabulary control (if any) that best serve it" (Woodley 2016, 9). Problems related to interoperability only appear when "a community shares content with others or wants to reuse the information for other purposes". In some contexts, information architects will continue to structure and organise information on behalf of their users; in others, they will design environments and tools that engage their users in folksonomic acts of co-creation (Morville et al. 2015).

Considering the different languages that currently constitute information architecture (audiovisual, iconographic, sound, and textual), tagging metadata also permit web documents to be processed with existing specific content extraction methods.

Metadata are always gaining more space and importance in

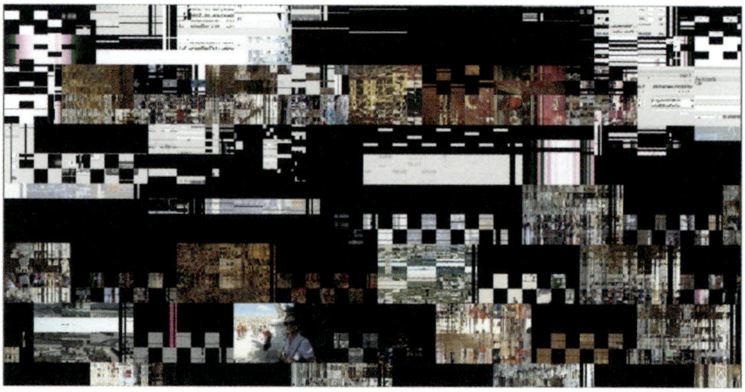

Figure 2 "Stack Disruption"
Source: www.mat.ucsb.edu/g.legrady/glWeb/Projects/sd/index.html

the configuration and conformation of our reality. Manovich (2002) explains that creating metadata is a new paradigm for interfacing reality and human experience. Manovich, an expert in new media language, is leading an interesting project focusing on new ways of describing and organising a considerable number of visual records about human experiences, and new interfaces and images.

Figure 2 shows a screenshot from the "Stack Disruption" project by George Legrady (2016), which consists of a set of images whose aesthetic properties are a direct result of errors occurring in the translation process of visualising an image file on the screen from its stored file format.

Conclusion

All these experiences are part of a new reality that is more complex and articulated than ever, and where sensors, data, algorithms and tags coexist with people from most cities in the world (there is still a huge digital divide in that only a third of the world's population have access to the network and digital devices), articulating and reforming cultures towards a scenario that has yet to be imagined.

References

Baca, M. (2016). *Introduction to Metadata*, Los Angeles: Getty Research Institute.

Doctor, G. R. S. (2007). *Understanding Metadata*. The Icfai Journal of Information Technology.

Gilliland, A. (2016). *Setting the Stage*, Los Angeles: Getty Research Institute.

Golder, S. A. & B. A. Huberman (2006). Usage patterns of collaborative tagging systems. *Journal of Information Science*, 32(2), 198–208.

Hedden, H. (2010). *The Accidental Taxonomist*, Medford, NJ: Information Today.

Manovich, L. (2002). *Metadata Mon Amour*. manovich.net/index.php/projects/metadata-mon-amour. Accessed 4 November 2019.

Monreal, C. & I. Gil (2010). Possibilities and limitations of thesauri in comparison with other systems of knowledge organization: Folksonomies, taxonomies and ontologies. *Interamericana Bibliotecología Journal*, 33(2), 361–377.

Monnin, A., F. Limpens, D. Laniado & F. Gandon (2009). *Speech acts meet tagging: ice tag ontology*. academia.edu/19748587/Speech_acts_meet_tagging_NiceTag_ontology. Accessed 14 December 2019.

Weinberger D. (2007). *Tagging and Why it Matters*. Berkman Center Research Publication. ssrn.com/abstract=870594.

Woodley, M. (2016). Metadata Matters: Connecting People and Information. In Murtha Baca (ed.), *Introduction to Metadata*, 1–37. Los Angeles: Getty Research Institute.

Quintarelli, E., A. Resmini & L. Rosati (2006). *FaceTag: Integrating Bottom-up and Top-down. Classification in a Social Tagging System.* Conference: SWAP 2006 – Semantic Web Applications and Perspectives, Proceedings of the 3rd Italian Semantic Web Workshop, Scuola Normale Superiore, Pisa, Italy, 18–20 December, 2006. citeseerx.ist.psu.edu/viewdoc/download?doi=10.1.1.71.5687&rep=rep1&type=pdf. Accessed 20 September 2019.

Rosenfeld, L., P. Morville & J. Arango (2015). *Information Architecture: For the Web and Beyond*, Sebastopol, CA: O'Reilly Media.

Vander Wal, T. (2007). *Folksonomy*. vanderwal.net/folksonomy.html. Accessed 26 September 2019.

Reading book covers

Book selection strategies online

Arūnas Gudinavičius & Andrius Šuminas

This research is a continuation of the results analysis from an exploratory study that was conducted in 2015 and showed that the book choices of readers can at least partially be influenced by cover colour. The research question in this case is in whether some selection strategies and browsing patterns could be identified when readers are searching for books in digital bookstores, and whether these preferences change with age and between genders. One hundred and eighty respondents participated in the experiment and were studied using a mobile eye-tracking laboratory. The experiment revealed three different information-seeking and attention distribution strategies for book selection, and six different browsing patterns adopted by respondents who used the consistent selection strategy were identified. Also, when comparing genders, it was noticed that men paid considerably less attention to book covers, but not to textual information given below.

Introduction

In recent years, the massive growth in the number of books published suggests that many will remain unknown because of insufficient number of people will read them (Dixon et al. 2015). This problem means publishers have to think about how to attract a customer's attention to their books. A significant role is played by book covers, as a sort of 'bait' in the process of book selection. It is easy to find situations where readers choose a book by its cover: does this mean, when comparing several books with similar content, their covers could be the deciding factor? If someone is looking for a gift, can a nice cover be a deciding factor? Are readers prepared to spend more money on books with attractive covers?

In all these cases, we have to select a book from tens or even thousands of items, so we need to apply one or another book selection strategy and browsing pattern. This fact makes it important for the publisher to understand not only how to design an attractive book cover, but also what selection strategies and browsing patterns readers are using. Knowing which elements attract more of the readers' attention, what they see and what they do not, helps booksellers to decide how books should be placed on shelves (whether physical or virtual) to ensure the browsing and selection experience is easy and comfortable for the reader, with the result that books are sold more successfully.

Some researchers have investigated web search patterns. Lorigo et al. (2006) discovered that gender and task significantly influence search behaviours. Cutrell and Guan (2007) found that adding information to the contextual object significantly improved performance for informational tasks but degraded performance for navigational tasks. Nielsen (2006) discovered and analysed with Pernice (2017) one of the most common browsing patterns – the F-pattern. The present article is a continuation of the results analysis from an exploratory study that was conducted in 2015 and showed that the book choices of readers can at least partially be influenced by cover colour. It has also been found that preferences for cool or warm colours and the speed of decision does, to some degree, differ across genders and age groups (Gudinavičius & Šuminas 2017).

Here, we ask whether selection strategies and browsing patterns could be identified when readers are searching for books in digital bookstores. How do these strategies and patterns change with age and between genders?

Methodology

In order to see the respondents' reading (browsing) strategies and patterns, we used a mobile eye-tracking laboratory set up in a bookshop and later in a library. The experiment took place in Vilnius, Lithuania in June 2015. As we wanted to compare selection strategies and browsing patterns across genders and age groups, we had an equal number of participants in each group: there were 90 male and 90 female respondents, with 60 respondents in each age group (age 18–35, 36–55 and over 56). In total, 180 respondents participated in the experiment. All of them were random visitors of one of the biggest bookshops in Vilnius (Lithuania), so it is likely they were all book readers (and buyers, more or less).

A fictional webpage of a digital bookstore was created with 18 books, all listed at the same price. Covers were randomly selected from a book cover sample database according to specific rules: two covers from each colour category (predominantly warm: red-violet, red, red-orange, orange, yellow-orange, yellow; and cool: yellow-green, green, blue-green, blue, blue-violet, violet); an equal proportion of cover illustration categories (photorealistic images, paintings and cartoons); and an equal distribution of women, men, children, and natural landscapes as part of the cover art. While titles and authors' names (and their colours) offer a different type of information from the rest of a book jacket, they were considered parts of the cover along with any other textual or visual information. Afterwards, covers were distributed randomly across an online bookshop shelf composed of three rows and six columns. All books were in the Lithuanian language (originals or translations).

In order to minimize the chance of a respondent finding a book they had already read (with a title and author they are already familiar with), we did not use books that could be described as bestsellers, or books by well-known authors.

During the course of the experiment, we asked each respondent to choose one book they would like to have right now from our sample of 18 books, so that the browsing type, according Marchionini's (1995) classification, based on the object (information) of search and on the systematicity of tactics used, can be described as directed browsing (systematic, focused and directed by a specific target).

The time for selecting a book was not limited. For each book the respondents were presented with a thumbnail-sized book cover (which included titles and author names), along with a title, author and price (all prices were set to €2.90), stated underneath the cover as brief item descriptions. The respondents were informed in advance that it was not possible to get more information by clicking on a specific cover. A fictional online bookstore bookshelf was presented on a large laptop (19-inch) monitor (Figure 1).

The respondents' basic gazing data (focus points, entry points, reading paths, time spent) was gathered using a mobile eye-tracking laboratory: a Tobii X2-30 Eye Tracker with Tobii Studio 3.2 software installed on it and an I-VT fixation filter with a velocity threshold of 20 ms. The minimum fixation duration was set to 60 ms, and the adjacent fixations were merged if they did not exceed 75 ms and an angle of 0.5 degrees between fixations.

Information-seeking processes on screens can take a long time. As the time limit for selecting the book was not limited, we decided to use just the first 14 seconds (one third of the

Figure 1 Setup of the experiment in a bookstore in Vilnius, Lithuania Public domain

average time respondents took to make a decision) of gaze plots in order to have clearer visual data for analysis (after a certain period of time, the gaze plots can become almost unreadable and unsuitable for quantitative analysis).

Results

The experiment revealed three different information-seeking and attention distribution strategies for book selection. During the process of gathering information about the books, some people (Figure 2) paid attention only to book covers (the so-called *cover is important* strategy), some only to textual information below the book covers (the author, title and price – the so-called *cover is not important* strategy), and some paid attention both to the graphical design of book covers and to relevant textual information (the so-called *mixed* strategy).

During the process of gathering information and selecting books, 55% of all participants in the experiment (Figure 3) used the mixed strategy, 40.6% paid attention only to book covers

Figure 2 Examples of the *cover is important* and *cover is not important* strategies
Public domain

(the so-called *cover is important* strategy), and as few as 4.4% focused only on textual information below the book covers (the so-called *cover is not important* strategy).

One of the most striking variables to correlate with the difference in seeking and selection strategies was gender. The main attention distribution and information-seeking strategy

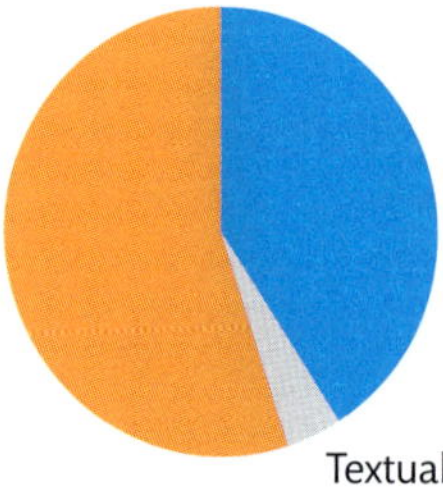

Figure 3 Information-seeking and attention distribution strategies

Table 1 Information-seeking and attention distribution strategies by gender

Gender	*Mixed*	*Book cover*	*Textual info*
Women	48.9%	50.0%	1.1%
Men	61.1%	31.1%	7.8%

Table 2 Information-seeking and attention distribution strategies by age

Age	*Mixed*	*Book cover*	*Textual info*
18–35	51.7%	40.0%	8.3%
36–55	63.3%	33.3%	3.3%
56+	50.0%	48.3%	1.7%

among women was the *cover is important* strategy – 50% of all women gathered information about the books only from their covers. The use of such a strategy among men was considerably lower – 31.1% of men paid attention to book covers only (Table 1). Meanwhile, a larger number of men used the mixed strategy – 48.9% – while 7.8% employed the *cover is not important* strategy. The number of women that used these strategies was distinctly lower – 48.9% used the mixed strategy and only 1.1% the *cover is not important* strategy.

Figure 4 Examples of *consistent* and *chaotic* selection strategies Public domain

Respondents' behaviour analyses conducted from the perspective of age allow us to notice young people's tendency to use the *cover is not important* strategy most often. The respondents in the 56+ age category tended to use the *cover is important* strategy more often than the respondents in other age groups (Table 2).

The respondents may also be categorized based on their gazing path – consistent vs. chaotic (Figure 4). A consistent selection strategy is characterised by a gazing path with a clear logic and structure. This means that people are consistently using a single path to scan elements on screen (e.g. going from left to right or from right to left of a screen; from top to bottom or from bottom to top, etc.).

A chaotic selection strategy is characterised by a gazing path without any clear logic or structure. People read information on different parts of the screen without clear paths, jumping from one element to another.

We found that the chaotic selection strategy is more commonly used – 57.8% of people used it, as opposed to 42.2% using the consistent selection strategy.

We observed that gender appeared to have little influence on selection strategies. Among the female respondents, 56.7% used the chaotic and 43.3% the consistent selection strategies. Respectively, 58.9% of men browsed in the chaotic and 41.1% in the consistent way (Table 3).

We found that age had a marked impact on respondents' behaviour: older people browsed in a more chaotic manner, while the younger ones were more consistent. Among the 18–35 age group, the chaotic selection strategy was used by only 43.3% of the respondents; in the 35–55 age group the figure rose to 53.3%, and among the 56+-year-olds, it was 76.7%. Conversely, 56.7% of the 18–35 age group used the consistent selection strategy, 46.7% of the 36–55 age group, and only 23.3% from the 56+ age group (Table 4).

Nielsen (2006) discovered the so-called 'F-shaped pattern', stating that internet users often read Web pages in this pattern: two horizontal stripes followed by a vertical stripe. Pernice (2017), revisiting the study, added that scanning on the web does not always take the shape of an F; there are other common scanning patterns too.

Table 3 Selection strategies by gender

Gender	*Chaotic*	*Consistent*
Women	56.7%	43.3%
Men	58.9%	41.1%

Table 4 Selection strategies by age

Age	*Chaotic*	*Consistent*
18–35	43.3%	56.7%
36–55	53.3%	46.7%
56+	76.7%	23.3%

It has been observed that the F-pattern is negative for users and for businesses alike, because users may skip important content simply because it appears on the wrong side of the page. In responsive design, text flows differently depending on window size. A user who scans in an F-shape on his phone, for example, would not fixate on the same words if he F-scanned the same page on a desktop, simply because of the way the content flows in different viewport sizes.

One of our tasks was to identify the browsing patterns that users employed while selecting books through the digital bookstore. Among the 180 respondents who took part in our research, 76 used the consistent selection strategy. In order to identify the most common of these consistent browsing patterns, we analysed those 76 cases, observing the gaze plots of the first 14 seconds of each respondent.

We distinguished six different browsing patterns adopted by respondents who used the consistent selecting strategy (Figure 5).

We found that the most frequently used browsing patterns

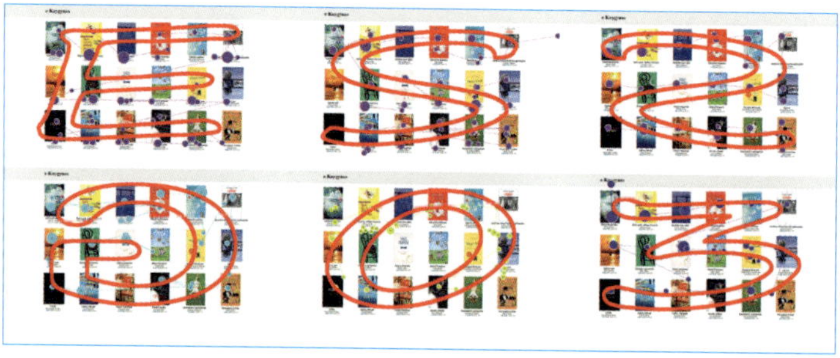

Figure 5 Examples of different browsing patterns Public domain

were the reverse S-pattern (44.7%) and the E-pattern (22.4%). Other browsing patterns appeared more rarely: the reverse G-pattern (11.8%), the 3-pattern (10.5%), the S-pattern and the O-pattern, each accounting for 5.3% of all cases (Table 5). The fact that we saw no F-patterns might be due to the specific nature of our content. We provided 18 book covers distributed symmetrically into three rows and six columns. Nevertheless, the E-pattern, which was amongst the most frequently used, is similar in form to the F-pattern.

Conclusion

To conclude, we are aware of the fact that the limitations of our study, especially the size of the respondent sample, does not allow us to generalise our results; despite this, we may outline some tendencies. The graphical elements of book information draw a lot of attention regardless of the gender or age of the viewer. The number of people who concentrate only on textual information is minimal. Here we should not forget that the readers' aim was to choose one book they would like from the samples provided. We also observed correlations regarding the use of either consistent or chaotic selection strategies with age: the older the respondents, the more visible was the tendency to adopt the chaotic selection strategy. This issue requires a more in-depth study, but we suppose that this observation may be explained by different levels of familiarity with digital information sources. Young people are accustomed to gathering information from digital sources, so they have more developed, distinct patterns for browsing information presented on screens.

It was noticed that men paid considerably less attention than women to book covers, but not to textual information displayed below them. In analysing age groups, we noticed that respondents from older age groups tended to use the *cover is important* strategy more often than the group of younger respondents. Our research also confirmed that the F-pattern is neither the sole nor the most important pattern for scanning a page, and that browsing patterns used may depend on the content itself, the distribution across the screen, and the viewer's aims.

At the beginning of our research, we assumed that people who pay attention to textual information (the *mixed* and *textual information* strategies) would be more likely to adopt a consistent selection strategy, as reading text imposes linear behaviour on acquiring information. Although our research did not confirm the existence of such a correlation, the tendencies discovered may be useful for publishers in order to better understand readers' behaviour when selecting books online.

Acknowledgements

This research took place at and was funded by the Digital Media Lab at the Faculty of Communication, Vilnius University. We are grateful to Justinas Červokas for the collection and statistical analysis of the eye-tracking data and Ingrida Kuorytė for managing the respondents.

References

Cutrell, E. & Z. Guan (2007). What are you looking for? *Proceedings of the SIGCHI Conference on Human Factors in Computing Systems – CHI '07*, 407–416. New York, NY: ACM Press.

Dixon, P., M. Bortolussi & B. Mullins (2015). Judging a book by its cover. *Scientific Study of Literature*, 5(1), 23–48.

Gudinavičius, A. & A. Šuminas (2018). Choosing a book by its cover: Analysis of a reader's choice. *Journal of Documentation*, 74(2), 430–446.

Lorigo, L., B. Pan, H. Hembrooke, T. Joachims, L. Granka & G. Gay (2006). The influence of task and gender on search and evaluation behavior using Google. *Information Processing & Management*, 42(4), 1123–1131.

Marchionini, G. (1997). *Information Seeking in Electronic Environments*, Cambridge: Cambridge University Press.

Nielsen, J. (2006). *F-Shaped Pattern For Reading Web Content (original study)*. Accessed 10 September 2019. nngroup.com/articles/f-shaped-pattern-reading-web-content-discovered.

Pernice, K. (2017). F-Shaped pattern of reading on the Web: Misunderstood, but still relevant (even on mobile). Accessed 10 September 2019. nngroup.com/articles/f-shaped-pattern-reading-web-content.

The materiality of support materials (informal books) in the classroom

The hidden world of materials crafted by teachers

Ann Marcus-Quinn & Triona Hourigan

This brief paper will explore the comfort and reassurance offered by the book as an object in the classroom. In Ireland, the National Council for Curriculum and Assessment (NCCA) recognises that the presentation of creative work and writing is crucial to the development of reading skills. The NCCA states that it is crucial that children with language and reading difficulties are identified as early as possible and given the necessary remedial support. Due to a lack of financial resources teachers are often required to craft their own support materials and these frequently take the form of a hardcopy book or pamphlet. The type of book produced by teachers in this environment may be seen as 'informal'. The familiarity offered by the physical structure of the traditional book affords this weaker group of students the scaffolding necessary to work with text in a way that is not overwhelming. This paper will describe the informal books that many teachers in this situation create for their students, and discuss why this is an attractive option for engaging this type of student.

Introduction

Technology has become embedded in the everyday practices of many schools, which use a range of technologies to support teaching and learning. The role of the teacher is seen as imperative to the process of developing ICT and digital literacy skills in the next generation and steps are being taken to ensure that teachers receive the support that they need to carry out this vital role. This drive is evident in a number of countries. More than a decade ago, in December 2008 the Dutch Minister of Education announced the Wikiwijs project (wikiwijs.nl), an open, internet-based platform, where teachers can find, download, (further) develop and share educational resources.

The project is based on open source software, open content and open standards. Wikiwijs is inspired by the idea of wikis: collaborative developing of content. Educational resources are developed by teachers, for teachers. Teachers can freely use anything they find in the Wikiwijs database in their classrooms. Wikiwijs is available to all levels of the Dutch educational system: primary, post-primary and third level. This project showed the commitment of the Dutch government to implementing a clearly defined and realistic approach to incorporating ICT into the post-primary classroom. It also highlighted the commitment of the government to supporting the development of suitable resources for teachers and students. There have been other similar efforts across the globe, such as MIT's Open Courseware to promote the uptake of Open Education.

In 2015, Schuwer and Wild (2015) declared that the pioneering phase of such projects "has come to an end" and that the impact of such projects can now be analysed in order to identify the impediments to large-scale adoption of open education.

Such initiatives have also drawn attention to the technologies that can facilitate development work. In the past, rapid authoring tools and dissemination systems were unavailable to ICT initiatives. Now software, such as Articulate or Raptivity, allows for rapid development of classroom materials by non-technical experts for delivery on smart devices and tablets. In Europe there has been much activity in the area of ICT in schools at all levels and in all sectors of education. Numerous reports have been commissioned on ICT provision and access, and more specifically on the importance of digital literacy to today's students. In a relatively short period of time, ICT skills have become as fundamental to living a full life as being able to read and write. There is a growing body of evidence on the positive impact that ICT can have on the learning of pupils with special educational needs, whether through adaptive or assistive technologies specially designed to support pupils with specific disabilities or through the use of mainstream technologies such as digital video and photography. Where does this focus on technology leave the traditional book?

Many teachers acknowledge that there is a need to recognise the growing importance of digital resources for the classroom, particularly where the digital format may appear to be more accessible than the dense form of printed text. However, there is some apprehension that where students have access to a treasure trove of information online many may not have the ability to engage with the material in a meaningful manner, or to and understand the information beyond a superficial level. There have also been concerns raised around memory and recall when digital materials have replaced traditional hardcopy. Schilhab et al. (2018) state that "whereas printed text affords numerous stable material anchors in the moment for memorizing, digital texts are much reduced in this respect".

In Ireland, the Junior Certificate English curriculum is varied and expects that all students will develop their language and literacy skills. One of its main aims is to reinforce and continue the work of the primary school in nurturing the intellectual, imaginative and emotional growth of each student by developing his/her personal proficiency in the arts and skills of language.

The guidelines are not prescriptive. Each individual teacher is free to choose his or her preferred teaching method for the achievement of the specified objectives and desired outcomes of each new syllabus. These guidelines do offer some suggestions which may be of further help to teachers.

However, the Junior Certificate English has undergone a lot of change in the last three years. There is a new curriculum, but it still requires that students sitting both the higher and ordinary level examination will be examined on the following:

- Reading
- Writing
- Functional Writing
- Media Studies
- Drama (unseen and studied)
- Poetry
- Fiction

In this new Junior Certificate classroom, teachers are also encouraged to explore new methods of teaching. The many Subject Inspection Reports available online advocate innovative teaching and recognise the schools that teach beyond the textbook. There is an emerging expectation that teachers will not only incorporate more digital resources into their teaching practice but also that they will become producers of such digital content (Banks et al. 2018; Ganapathy, Wei & Jong 2015). However, many teachers do not have training in the design and development of digital resources (Akpinar & Simsek 2007; Baytak & Hirca 2013).

As a result, many design features can be overlooked and classroom resources may not be as effective as anticipated. In these Subject Inspection Reports we can also see that some teachers choose not to use a set textbook with their classes, opting instead for an 'informal' book. An 'informal' book in this context may have a number of guises. Some teachers may craft their own photocopied teaching materials into the form of a traditional softbound book. Anecdotally, some teachers create their own booklets comprising the chosen ten poems for an academic year. Each student is given a copy of this little booklet. Such bespoke materials are often seen as a means of motivating the students. Some teachers find that there is a lack of curriculum-relevant material, particularly for students at the lower levels.

Some teachers find that designing their own informal booklet enables them to furnish their students with a 'book' that does not overwhelm or intimidate. These books may not incorporate traditional access devices such as a table of contents or an index. The teacher may limit the content, choosing not to include extensive questions on the core text. The book may instead cover the bare essentials for a teacher's lesson plan, guided by the ability and reading level of their class. For example, a teacher delivering a lesson on poetry may photocopy content from the core textbook that is being used with the more able students, omitting all of the questions and notes on the poem. Instead, they might present the poem on its own or with a graphic beside the text to try to engage the students without overwhelming them. Some teachers creating informal books in this manner will also ensure that there is a lot of white space on each page so that the students are free to annotate the poem themselves as it is discussed in class.

While there is some limited reporting of the production of handmade content, including books, in the literature (Moore 1986; Ikuta et al. 2012) it is very difficult to capture the number of teachers engaging in this work; this kind of activity is under-reported for a variety of reasons. For example, teachers may not share the booklets and the number of teachers involved in writing and publishing their classroom practice in academic journals and presenting at academic conferences is also minimal. Therefore, many innovative creative teaching practices that take place are not captured in the literature.

There are reports online of teachers creating books to bring creativity to the curriculum and to engage with weaker students. The website Making Books (makingbooks.com) provides many first-hand teacher accounts of teachers creating books, sometimes on their own and sometimes with the children that they teach.

Over the years I've worked to make bookmaking as easy as possible. I now use repurposed materials as much as possible which saves preparation time. I don't get hung up about precision and perfection. The more joy in the process, the more books you and your students will want to make. The more books they make, the more writing and learning will happen. (Gaylord 2016)

Brown and Towell (2015) also extol the virtues of engaging younger students (primary school level) in the creation of books for use in their classrooms. Much of the literature around such book production concerns early childhood education and there are very few accounts describing handmade books either by teachers or pupils beyond this stage of education. The exception is in creative subjects such as Art (Strauch-Nelson 2011), where book-making is recognised as "a powerful and holistic means of engaging students physically, emotionally, socially, and intellectually". However, there are still very few accounts of such activity at post-primary level. Anecdotally we can see that teachers agree that personalised learning in today's contemporary classroom, with students at the centre of all activity, can be a positive experience for all stakeholders, but there are challenges that must be overcome.

With the New Junior Cycle the content of the curriculum has been 'reduced' and interestingly the textbooks currently being produced are much less detailed in terms of content. The NCCA wants all teachers to produce their own materials to supplement textbooks, since there are no set areas to cover. Scoilnet.ie is the Department of Education and Skills' (DES) official portal for Irish education. Originally launched in 1998, the website is managed by PDST Technology in Education on behalf of the DES. Scoilnet collaborates with practising teachers to maintain and manage the content on the website. The Department of Education is also encouraging teachers to use Scoilnet. It has been developed as a support for teachers at both primary and post-primary levels and, since 2014, provides teachers with the option to share and upload their own teaching and learning resources.

This approach is aimed at students of all ranges of ability. What will probably happen is that teachers will start photocopying notes from other books, which will then be lost by less organised students. This is their attempt to 'encourage' collaboration between teachers, but whether that is achievable remains to be seen. Some schools are also 'writing' their own textbooks, but this only seems to be prevalent where students have all been required to invest in iPads. Such book-writing might be seen as a way to reduce costs for parents investing in technology. Students in some subjects also have to produce their own portfolios of work, which is another dimension in the role of informal books.

Conclusion

For many weaker students support materials are critical and tailored materials developed by teachers enable learning to happen. Support materials delivered in a digital format are 'headline grabbing', and work with eLearning and digital materials will always capture the public's attention. Teachers' work with hardcopy materials such as informal books does not seem to attract the same positive coverage in school evaluations, subject inspection reports or the media. Teacher activities in the area of materials production are thus under-reported and under-supported. Teachers themselves value informal books and it is time that these resources were recognised in some formal capacity in school evaluations and subject inspection reports. Only when there is such recognition of this type of book can the true value and role of the informal book be recognised as an important aspect of classroom activity.

References

Akpinar, Y. & H. Simsek (2007). Should K-12 teachers develop learning objects? Evidence from the field with K-12 students. *International Journal of Instructional Technology and Distance Learning*, 4(3), 31–44.

Banks, J., S. MacCoy & E. Smyth (2018). *Senior Cycle Review: Analysis of discussions in schools on the purpose of senior cycle education in Ireland*. ESRI Working Paper 607.

Baytak, A. & N. Hirca (2013). Prospective teachers' lived experience on computer-based instructional materials: A phenomenological study. *The Anthropologist*, 16(1–2), 97–109.

Brown, S. & J. L. Towell (2015). Engaging young writers through book design. *Kappa Delta Pi Record*, 51(4), 185–189.

Ganapathy, M., V. C. P. Wei & C. J. Jong (2015). Teachers' perceptions of creating, sharing and using Open Education Resources (OERs) in Universiti Sains Malaysia (USM). *International Journal of e-Education, e-Business, e-Management and e-Learning*, 5(2), 62.

Gaylord, S. K. (2016). *Making Books*. makingbooks.com.

Ikuta, S., F. Nemoto, E. Endo, S. Kaiami, K. Fukushima & T. Ezoe (2012). Handmade Teaching Materials and School Activities with New Dot-codes Handling Multimedia. *Proceedings of SITE 2012: Society for Information Technology & Teacher Education International Conference*. Association for the Advancement of Computing in Education (AACE).

Marcus-Quinn, A. & O. McGarr (2013). Digital divide in post-primary schools. *Internet in the Humanities: An Insight from Ireland*, (pp. 277–303). Dublin: ResearchPublishing.net.

Moore, B. (1986). Literacy and children's books in the South Pacific region. *Directions: Journal of Educational Studies*, 8(2), 5–10.

Schuwer, R. & U. Wild (2015). Beyond the pioneering phase: Moving towards the adoption of open education. *Open and Online Education Trend Report*. Available at: https://www.researchgate.net/profile/Renee_Filius/publication/284182930_Trend_report_Open_and_Online_Education_2015/links/564ef56108aefe619b10cf16/Trend-report-Open-and-Online-Education-2015.pdf#page=9.

Schilhab, T., G. Balling & A. Kuzmicova (2018). Decreasing materiality from print to screen reading. *First Monday*, 23(10).

SCOILNET. scoilnet.ie.

Strauch-Nelson, W. J. (2011). Book learning: The cognitive potential of bookmaking. Teaching Artist Journal, 9(1), 5– 15.

The materiality of textbooks

From black-and-white textbooks to the digital textbook ecosystem

Alenka Kepic Mohar

This article discusses changes in the materiality of textbooks by examining several examples of primarily Slovenian textbooks from various periods. By focusing on their spread design rather than technical aspects (such as length, weight, and format) it can be concluded that their materiality changed with the development of printing technologies and publishing skills. Based on the assumption that textbook visuality is a field of meaning that requires different bodily movements, postures and engagement with the physical environment to create cognitive processing, this article sheds light on how the body adapts to the changed materiality of digital textbooks. Numerous micro-movements in a long string of procedures are required in a digital textbook ecosystem. All of this might be natural for generations of digital natives, for whom digital experience is embedded in their way of life; however, it should be reconciled with all participants in the educational process, including policymakers and the publishers of educational materials. Therefore, further empirical research is proposed.

Introduction

This article sheds light on how modern technology has changed the materiality of textbooks. Publishing studies, researchers of the history of books and the media only rarely pay attention to textbooks, owing to their prescribed characteristics and dependence on the educational system.

Textbook analysis is primarily an educational studies topic; however, it is usually focused on issues related to content, as well as teaching and learning methods, while the changing materiality of textbooks and its impact on education processes is largely overlooked. Moreover, although the transition from print to digital has crucially transformed the materiality of textbooks, it has been poorly researched, with studies focusing primarily on learning efficiency (for example Singer & Alexander 2017; Sidi et al. 2017). The impact of this transition from print to digital will be corroborated by Daniel Miller's (2011) anthropological theory of materiality and by the interdisciplinary paradigm of embodied cognition (Thelen et al. 2001; Wilson 2002; Shapiro 2010), which is rapidly gaining ground and is based on the discovery that cognitive processing is fundamentally dependent on the body, postures and bodily movements, as well as on our engagement with our physical environment and the ways in which we read and learn (McLaughlin 2015; Mangen 2016).

Theoretical framework

In his anthropological study of material culture, Miller (2016) argues that things make us just as much as we make things. This can be linked to Bourdieu's unconscious order or *habitus*: nature exists, but culture gives us our second nature – that which we do habitually without thinking. Things – or, more precisely, the whole system of things with their internal order –

make us who we are. One can, therefore, argue that textbooks, as elements of formal education and holders of symbolic value in the economy of cultural goods (Bourdieu 1993), also imperceptibly affect and shape us through their materiality. Miller's understanding of material culture can be narrowed down to an understanding of the book as an object and the practice of reading, which accord perfectly with Thomas McLaughlin's reasoning. In *Reading and the Body*, McLaughlin (2015) highlights the overlooked importance of bodily aspects of reading, which is not only a mental 'encounter' between the reader's mind and meanings of the text expressed through the author's voice but also a bodily act through which the book physically enters the reader's body.

According to McLaughlin (2015, 46), the graphic environment can be understood as a field of meaning, with units that must be comprehended, and as a field of play – a series of physically and cognitively efficient sites for landing and leaping. This raises questions regarding how changes in materiality affect physical tasks and habitual textbook-reading practices and usage, and how the reading experience changes when the purpose of reading is learning.

The changing materiality of textbooks

Printed textbooks have undergone extensive transformation in the last 40 years (Garcia 2015) as a result of new (editorial) production and printing technologies and the effort to make textbooks more compatible with other media. The most striking change is the increasing use of images, as well as the emergence of icons and/or other visual elements, highlighted spaces, different fonts and colours, and other kinds of graphic design resources that stimulate learning beyond the mere written text.

Regarding textbooks, computer-aided design accelerated production and increased content diversity, while new design, graphic and printing opportunities enhanced the role of visual elements. Diverse typography, different colour backgrounds and innovative graphic solutions opened the door to multilayered hierarchies of textbook content. Digitally accessible stock images simplified access to artwork, while computer illustration shortened and simplified its creation and production. All of these changes made textbooks more visually attractive. However, from the standpoint of materiality, the revolutionary change, comparable to the invention of printing, was catalysed by the transformation from printed to digital textbooks.

This changing materiality is illustrated below with several textbook spreads from various periods. These primarily Slovenian-language textbooks about ancient Greek history have been chosen to illustrate the differences in visuality. They were published in the 19th century (1871) (Figure 1), the first half of the 20th century (1938) (Figure 2), the end of the 20th century (1996) (Figure 3), and the beginning of the 21st century (2006) (Figure 5). The last figure shows an interactive textbook from 2018 (Figure 6).

The comparison of these three spreads yields interesting results if we take into account McLaughlin's statement (2016) that eye movement, book-holding manner, body posture, hand movement and page turning can be regarded as precognitive body activities. The eyes move down the page with strict kinetic discipline, and the hands follow them, holding the book in a way that enables the eyes to operate. Initially, this is done consciously but later automatically, allowing the reader to focus on cognitive activities.

Colourfulness, layout and typographic emphases are the features that differentiate the 1996 textbook (Figure 3) from the two older ones (Figures 1 and 2), which require a different operation of the eyes. The main text occupying the central two thirds of the page (Figure 3) is complemented by artwork in the outer margin. Consequently, the eyes no longer move smoothly

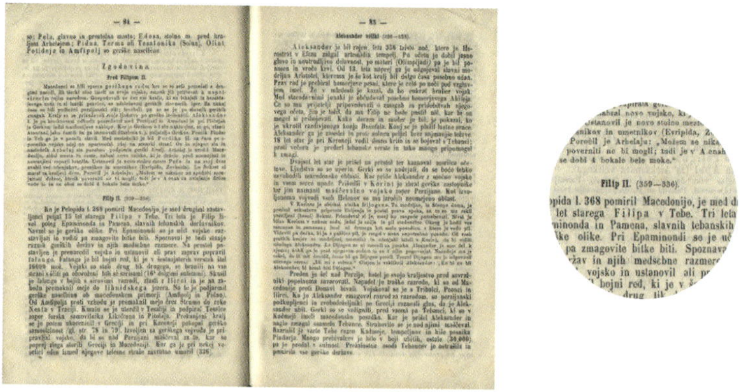

Figure 1 J. Jesenko, *Obča zgodovina za nižje razrede srednjih šol* (General History for Lower Secondary School Grades), 1871 Public domain

The content of the textbook by J. Jesenko *Obča zgodovina za niže razrede srednjih šol* (General History for Lower Secondary School Grades), from 1871, is divided into chapters and subchapters, emphasised words are printed in semi-bold or spaced type, and the leading is small. The size of the typography varies minimally, and the text is set in one compact column and divided linearly into paragraphs across the width of the entire page. The printing is in black and white, there are no photographs nor artwork, and the book is in A5, hardback format.

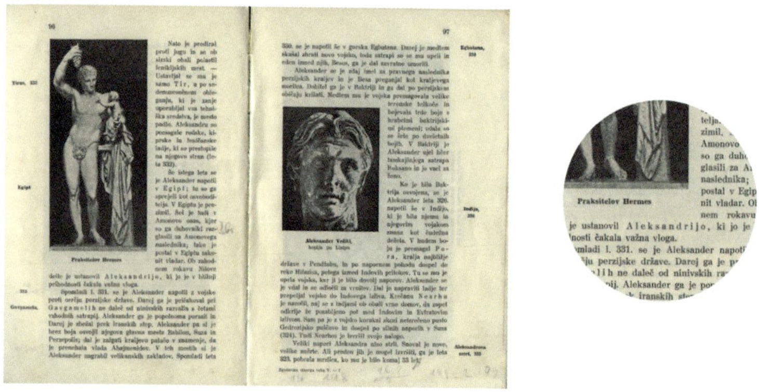

Figure 2 J. Orožen, *Zgodovina starega veka za V. razred srednjih šol* (History of Antiquity for Secondary School Grade V), 1938 Public domain

In the textbook by J. Orožen *Zgodovina starega veka za V. razred srednjih šol* (History of Antiquity for Secondary School Grade V), from 1938, printed in black and white, the text is set in one column but is interrupted by photographs and captions, and keywords and years appear in the outer margin. Emphasised words are printed in spaced or semi-bold type. The book is in A5, hardback format.

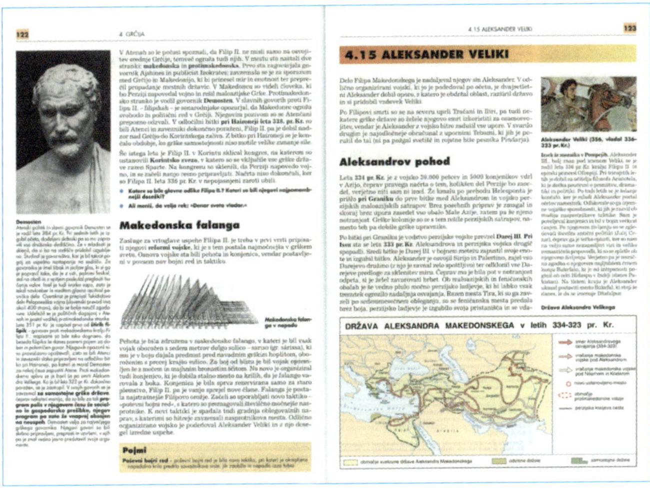
122
4 GRČIJA
Makedonska falanga
Pojmi
123
4.15 ALEKSANDER VELIKI
Aleksandrov pohod
DRŽAVA ALEKSANDRA MAKEDONSKEGA v letih 334-323 pr. Kr.

Figure 3 B. Repe, *Naša doba: Oris zgodovine 20. stoletja, učbenik za 4. razred gimnazije* (Our Age: An outline of 20th-century history, textbook for High School), DZS, 1996 Reprinted with permission

The paperback textbook by Repe (1996) is printed in four colours. Occupying two thirds of the page, the main text is complemented by photographs with extensive explanations, drawings and instructional coloured maps. Different typography is used to introduce various levels of text, which appear against the coloured background. The format is lowered A4, paperback.

across the width of the entire page. The reader instantly decides which block to read next, with reading order being partly dictated by typography. The illustrations and pictorial material activate different mental images, which are aligned with our internal model (Eagelman 2015, 60), and different manners of reading. Even if the path of the eyes changes owing to the visual aspect of the text and numerous elements that are no longer only textual, the operation of the hands and the eyes is still disciplined, harmonised and limited by the printed book.

Starting in the 1990s, textbooks were published with CDs or DVDs and later with QR codes (Figures 4 and 5). Consequently, the book as a physical object 'expanded', while its consumption

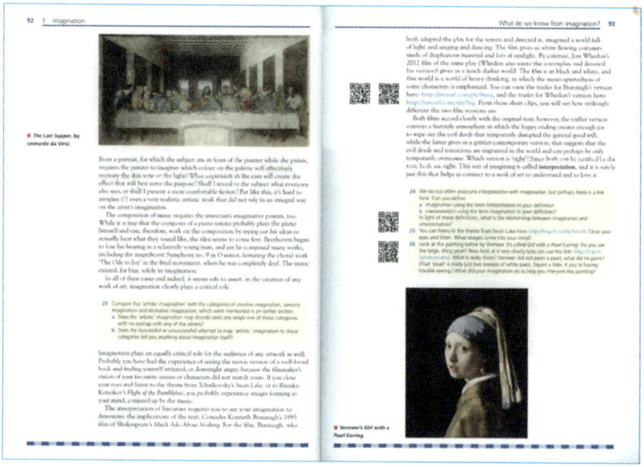
92 5 Imagination

The Last Supper, by Leonardo da Vinci

What do we know from imagination? 93

Vermeer's Girl with a Pearl Earring

Figure 4 N. Alchin and C. P. Henly, *Theory of Knowledge for the* IB *Diploma*, Hodder Education, 2006. A textbook with QR codes in the outer margins (Alchin et al. 2006) Reprinted with permission

required an additional medium – a CD/DVD player or smartphone – giving rise to different cognitive processes, bodily actions and haptic requirements. The reading process is thus interrupted, and the operation of the body during reading is affected by actions that no longer involve only micro-movements, such as holding the book, turning the pages and disciplining the eye movements. The reader leaves the book world to enter the external world of digital devices. The hands enable physical contact between the reader and the book. If the body participates in the reading process without mental instructions, as subtle but complex knowledge is immediately activated (McLaughlin 2015), a change in the focused attention and harmonised, disciplined operation of the hands and eyes occurs when dealing with content that has been expanded due to the enclosed multimedia. According to Hayles (2002, 23), "to change the material object is to transform the context and circumstances for interacting with the words, which inevitably changes the meanings of the words as well".

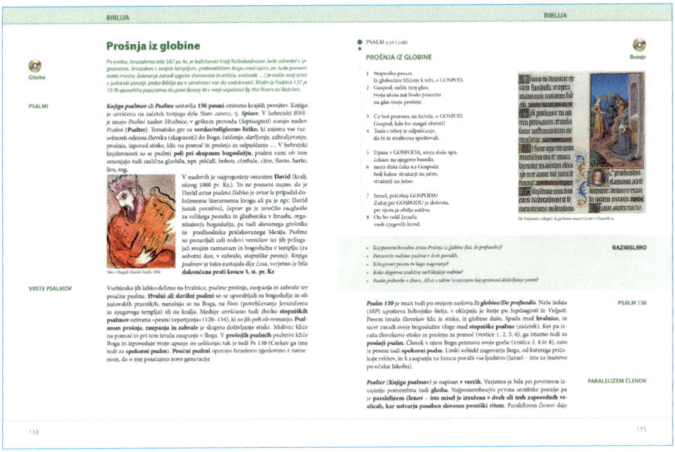
BIBLIJA

Prošnja iz globine

PSALMI

VRSTE PSALMOV

114

BIBLIJA

PROŠNJA IZ GLOBINE

RAZMISLIMO

PSALM 130

PARALELIZEM ČLENOV

115

Figure 5 K. Lah, B. Lenaršič, J. Perko, V. Matajc and M. Marinčič, *Berilo 1, Umetnost besede* (Reader 1, The Art of Words, Textbook for High School Grade 1), Mladinska knjiga, 2006 Reprinted with permission

Printed using the four-colour technique, the spread in Lenaršič et al.'s book from 2006 reveals artwork in the form of tables, keywords and collocations in the outer margin, and the main text is in black print. Key terms are in semi-bold type, the introductory motivational text is in coloured print, and the metadata are at the head and foot of the page. The outer margin displays icons as a guide to the enclosed DVD containing additional material, videos, music and so on. The format is lowered A4, paperback.

In the 2010s, digital textbooks existed in two different formats, the most common form by far being the page-fidelity or print-fidelity product: exact screen renderings of printed pages (see Figure 6). These products maintain the layout of the printed textbook and are most often built from PDF source files exported directly from the publisher's print workflow (Chesser 2014). Contrastingly, reflowable digital textbooks maintain all the contents from print textbooks but often strip away or dynamically deal with components of page layout. These products, which are typically constructed from XML instead of PDF source files, have fluid line and page breaks. Lines of text are wrapped and/or resized as viewing windows are adjusted or different devices mean readers to encounter various screen sizes. A reflowable e-textbook allows users to adjust font sizes and windows to their liking without resizing the entire page. Additionally, users can often designate their preferred background colours for pages, figures or box features.

Irrespective of their form, both types of digital textbooks place readers in a new environment – the so-called "docuverse" (van der Weel 2011) – in which they have to intuitively orient themselves and intelligently adjust the operation of their bodies and minds.

Before reading digital textbooks, users need to open them, meaning that they first have to use computers, tablets or smartphones to access the platforms on which the textbooks are published. The entrance protocol usually requires a registration procedure (i.e. entry of data and activation code). Having logged in, users choose the appropriate textbooks by clicking on them, thereby gaining access to spreads of printed textbooks. Sitting at the desktop computer and navigating with a mouse are physical procedures that demand intelligent adaptations to the rich materiality of the digital environment. According to McLaughlin (2015, 167), this requires an even higher degree of procedural intelligence than the codex reading experience.

Users need to accept cognitive, ocular and manual training to master the demands of technology. A wide range of subtle physical skills enables access to the virtual realm, and a set of precognitive activities is activated. Researchers have already analysed the effects of print size, scrolling features and ergonomic features on cognitive functioning (Stoop et al. 2013), as well as the comprehension and eye movements of participants reading from printed books, computer displays and handheld e-readers (Zambarbieri & Carniglia 2012). Additionally, research shows that navigational issues that arise while scrolling increase cognitive load (Singer & Aleksander 2017). Nevertheless, readers must be familiar with textbooks' digital architecture: in this case (Figures 6 and 7), the upper navigation bar with six functional buttons (menu, contents, note, highlight, share with school friends and teachers, and send answers) and the lower navigation bar, which enables users to move smoothly through the textbook (see below).

The enhanced text and figures are upgraded with icons in the margin or on the figures themselves. When they click on them, readers enter a new multimedia space. A complex muscular competence operates below the conscious awareness in the graphic space of the text (McLaughlin 2016, 46). We expect readers to take the following path: they will read the paragraph on Alexander the Great's conquests and then stop at the graphic

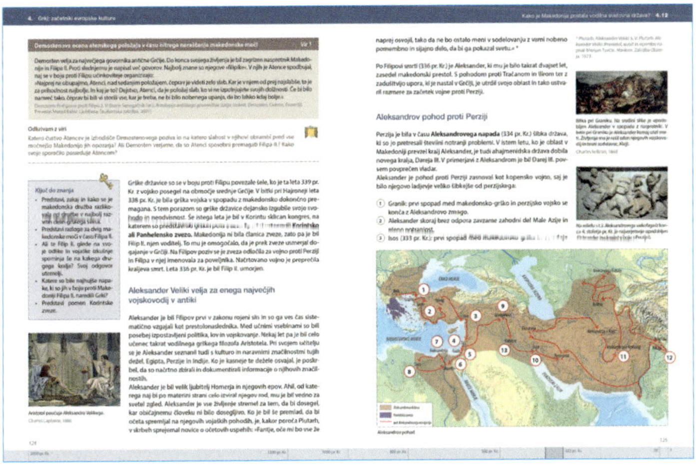

Figure 6 A. Cedilnik, G. Popovič Lozar, S. Škrlj Počkaj, M. Vičič Krabonja, M. Oblak, I. Paradižk, M: Kukanja-Gabrijelčič, *Zgodovina 1: Prazgodovina in antika* (History 1, Textbook for High School Grade 1), Mladinska knjiga, 2018, www.iucbenikimk.si Reprinted with permission

The interactive textbook by Cedilnik et al. from 2018 is designed in the page fidelity format. In addition to the icon which shows the interactive map when clicked on, the format is enlarged by the upper and lower navigation toolbars that place it in the digital environment and enable users to share notes, write footnotes, highlight text, send answers to teachers and so on.

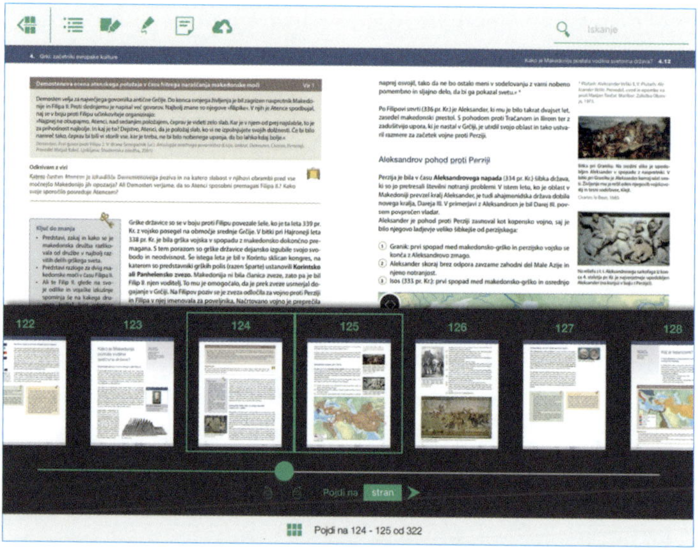

Figure 7 A. Cedilnik, G. Popovič Lozar, S. Škrlj Počkaj, M. Vičič Krabonja, M. Oblak, I. Paradižk, M: Kukanja-Gabrijelčič, *Zgodovina 1: Prazgodovina in antika* (History 1, Textbook for High School Grade 1), Mladinska knjiga, 2018, www.iucbenikimk.si Reprinted with permission

The navigation bar at the bottom enables users to move smoothly from page to page

representation of his battle marches, which is upgraded with an icon for interactive content. The reader's body is active: readers move the mouse on its pad, unconsciously monitoring how their hand movements create analogous movements on the screen. A tiny movement of the mouse creates an analogous movement on the screen, followed by a pause lasting only a few milliseconds before the pop-up window appears and opens the interactive map with a task to be completed. Intuitively looking for possible ways to answer it, readers select full-page view, complete the task and then return to the main page by pressing the button.

The double-layered world – the explanatory text and communicative environment of multimedia content (i.e. interactive questions and answers, films, and links) – creates two reading levels. For example, readers read the text on Alexander the Great's battle marches and then click on the icon on the map, only to find themselves in a completely new interactive environment. Their perceptions of what they have just read and the disciplined movements of their eyes and hands have to give way to precise micro clicks of the mouse; consequently, their opinions recede into the background, replaced by expectations of what kind of content will appear on the screen. Switching between the two environments – the static environment of the text and figures on the one hand, and the multimedia interaction on the other – requires new somatic capacities. It also affects the spasmodic way of reading.

Readers hop from point to point – what Wolf calls the "grasshopper mind" (2018, 108) – causing deviation from the circuit of deep reading, which, according to Wolf's findings (2018, 64–66), also involves analytical and generative processes. The messages of the text enable the creation of the inner space for reflection, for the so-called quiet eye (Dunn, quoted in Wolf 2018, 78), and for the emergence of inestimable thoughts that occasionally irradiate our consciousness with brief, luminous glimpses of what lies outside the boundaries of all we thought before (Wolf 2018, 66). Contrastingly, switching between the two environments, which is comparable to multitasking, diverts attention, weakens cognitive patience and encourages technological rather than phenomenological immersion (Mangen 2008, 406). Moreover, some empirical studies have proven that for longer texts, digital natives obtained better comprehension scores for print than digital reading (Davis & Neitzel 2012; Mangen et al. 2013).

Naturally, one cannot avoid the question of whether textbook reading inevitably requires multitasking, as learning often involves holding a pencil and taking notes, which increases the importance of the process of inner reflection on and 'digestion' of what is read. The question of how we read is also related to the individualisation of reading and learning; however, irrespective of our personal choice, this raises a further question that is linked to the mission of textbooks as a form of books but which goes beyond the scope of this article: how do new haptic requirements and changes in cognitive processes affect in-depth understanding and long-term knowledge?

Conclusion

The aim of this article was to discuss changes in the materiality of textbooks by examining several examples of primarily Slovenian textbooks from various periods. In focusing on their spread design, it can be concluded that their materiality changed with the development of printing technologies and publishing skills. Based on the assumption that textbook visuality is a field of meaning that requires different bodily movements, postures and engagement with the physical environment to create cognitive processing, this article shed light on how the body adapts to the changed materiality of textbooks. As illustrated, numerous micro-movements in a long string of procedures are demanded in a digital textbook ecosystem. This might be natural for generations of digital natives, for whom digital experience is embedded in their way of life, but it should be reconciled with all participants in the educational process, including policymakers and the publishers of educational materials.

Nevertheless, further empirical research is needed to address numerous unanswered questions: (1) How do new haptic requirements affect the formation of students' cognition? (2) How do these requirements change established learning techniques? (3) How can new haptic requirements be combined with task-inherent cues to avoid shallow processing and achieve the expected depth of processing as emphasized by cognitive and metacognitive researchers (Sidi et al. 2017)? (4) Bearing in mind that, in creating digital materials, processes need to be done more intuitively – can more bottom-up aspects be included to improve the efficiency of digital textbooks, as proposed by Schilhab (2015, Schilhab et al., 2018)?

Finally, the changed materiality of textbooks involves more than simply renaming the signifier; it involves a reinterpretation of meaning and evolutionary changes in the teaching and learning processes and, therefore, has a significant impact on shaping our future. For all of these reasons, our changing society must give this area the full research attention it deserves, taking into consideration all of its different aspects.

References

Alchin, N. (2006). *Theory of Knowledge*, Diploma: Hodder Education.

Bourdieu, P. (1993). *The Field of Cultural Production*, London, Cambridge: Polity Press.

Braga G. & M. F. Tânia (2015). From Print to Digital. In J. Rodríguez, E. Bruillard & M. Horsley (eds.), *Digital Textbooks: What's New?*, Santiago de Compostela: IARTEM.

Chesser, W. D. (2011). The e-textbook revolution. In S. Polanka (ed.), *The no shelf required guide to eBook purchasing. Library Technology Reports*, 47(8), 28–40.

Cedilnik, A. (2018). *Zgodovina 1, Prazgodovina in antika.* Ljubljana: Mladinska knjiga Publishing House.

Davis, D. S. & C. Neitzel (2012). Collaborative sense-making in print and digital text environments. *Reading and Writing*, 25(4), 831–856.

Eagelman, D. (2015). *The Brain: The Story of You*, Edinburgh: Canongate Books.

Hayles, N. K. (2002). *Writing Machines*, Cambridge: MIT Press.

Lenaršič et al. (2006). *Berilo 1*, Umetnost besede, Ljubljana: Mladinska knjiga Publishing House.

Orožen, J. (1938). *Zgodovina starega veka za V. razred srednjih šol* (History of Antiquity for Secondary School Grade V), Ljubljana: Merkur Press.

Mangen, A. (2016). Pen or Keyboard in Beginning Writing Instruction? Some Perspectives from Embodied Cognition. *Trends in Neuroscience and Education*, 5, 99–106.
Mangen, A., B. R. Walgermo & K. Brønnick (2013). Reading Linear Texts on Paper versus Computer Screen: Effects on Reading Comprchension. *International Journal of Educational Research*, 58, 61–68.
McLaughlin, T. (2015). *Reading and the Body*, New York: Palgrave Macmillan.
Miller, D. (2010). *Stuff*, Cambridge: Polity Press.
Repe, B. (1996). *Naša doba: Oris zgodovine 20. stoletja, učbenik za 4. razred gimnazije*, DZS.
Schilhab, T. (2015). Re-Live and Learn: Interlocutor-Induced Elicitation of Phenomenal Experiences in Learning Offline. *Progress in Biophysics and Molecular Biology*, 119, 649–660.
Shapiro, L. (2010). *Embodied Cognition*, London: Routledge.
Sidi, Y., M. Shpigelman, H. Zalmanov & R. Ackerman (2017). Understanding metacognitive inferiority on screen by exposing cues for depth of processing. *Learning and Instruction*, 51, 61–73.
Singer, L. M. & P. A. Alexander (2017). Reading across mediums: Effects of reading digital and print texts on comprehension and calibration. *Journal of Experimental Education*, 85(1), 155–172.
Stoop, J., P. Kreutzer & J. Kircz (2013). Reading and learning from screens versus print: A study in changing habits: Part 1. *New Library World*, 114, 284–300.
Thelen, E., G. Schöner, C. Scheier & L. B. Smith (2001). The dynamics of embodiment: A field theory of infant perseverative reaching. *Behavioral and Brain Science*, 24(1), 1–86.
van der Weel, A. (2011). *Changing Our Textual Minds. Towards a Digital Order of Knowledge*, Manchester: Manchester University Press.
Wilson, M. (2002). Six views on embodied cognition. *Psychonomic Bulletin & Review*, 9(4), 625–636.
Wolf, M. (2018). *Reader, Come Home: The Reading Brain in a Digital World*, New York: Harper Collins.
Zambarbieri, D. & E. Carniglia (2012). Eye movement analysis of reading from computer displays, eReaders, and printed books. *Ophthalmic and Physiological Optics*, 32, 390–396.

Authors

Chloé Aubry

PhD student, 3L.AM Laboratory, Le Mans University

Book materiality, artist's books, print culture, reading experience

Patrícia Dias

Assistant Professor, Research Centre for Communication and Culture, Catholic University of Portugal

Digital technologies, smartphones, young children, digital media, mobile marketing, mediation

Wayne de Fremery

Associate Professor, Sogang University

Bibliography, poetry, Korean literature, design, information science, artificial intelligence

Arūnas Gudinavičius

Associate professor, PhD, Digital Media Lab, Faculty of Communication, Vilnius University

Digital reading, e-books, publishing statistics, digital divide, eye tracking

Claire Gauzente

Professor, LEMNA, University of Nantes

Print and book studies, research methodology, ICT, subjective inquiry

Tríona Hourigan

PhD, Department of Education and Skills, Ireland

ICT in education, curriculum design, technology and second language acquisition

Arthur Jacobs

Professor, PhD, Experimental and Neurocognitive Psychology Unit, Dahlem Institute for Neuroimaging of Emotion (DINE), Center for Cognitive Neuroscience Berlin (CCNB), Free University of Berlin

Neuroimaging, learning, language, memory, fiction, poetry, executive functions

Anežka Kuzmičová

PhD, Faculty of Arts, Charles University

Literacy, embodied cognition, reading behaviour, reading for pleasure, education

Gerhard Lauer

Professor, PhD, Digital Humanities Lab, University of Basel

Literary history, digital humanities, reading science

Valeria Levratto

Lecturer, PhD, Faculty of Communication, Rey Juan Carlos University

Digital reading, media education and digital literacy, digital divide

Jana Lüdtke

Lecturer, PhD, Experimental and Neurocognitive Psychology Unit, Dahlem Institute for Neuroimaging of Emotion (DINE), Center for Cognitive Neuroscience Berlin (CCNB), Free University of Berlin

Reading research

Ann Marcus-Quinn

Lecturer, PhD, University of Limerick

Technical Communication, Instructional Design, ICT in Schools, Language Learning, OERs

Alenka Kepic Mohar

Head of Educational Department at Mladinska knjiga Publishing House, PhD, Department of Library and Information Science and Book Studies, Faculty of Arts, University of Ljubljana

Textbooks, digital textbooks, reading, educational publishing, education

Adrian Netedu

Professor, PhD, Faculty of Philosophy and Social-Political Sciences, Alexandru Ioan Cuza University

Sociological theory, sociological methodology, social statistics

Skans Kersti Nilsson

Docent, Department of Literature, History of Ideas, and Religion, Gothenburg University

Literature, sociology of literature, empirical studies of literature, reading research, media studies

Federico Pianzola

Marie Skłodowska Curie Research Fellow, University of Milan-Bicocca and Sogang University

Digital humanities, narrative theory, Italian literature, digital social reading, VR

Massimo Salgaro

Professor, PhD, University of Verona

Empirical aesthetics, digital humanities, literary theory

Theresa Schilhab

Associate Professor, Dr.pæd., PhD, Danish School of Education, University of Aarhus

Cognitive- and evo-neurobiology, embodied cognition, material culture, experiental learning

Pasqualina Sorrentino

PhD student, Geörg August University Göttingen

Cognitive literature, literary reading in the era of digitalization

Paul Stiff

Former professor, Department of Typography & Graphic Communication, University of Reading

Design for reading, information design

Andrius Šuminas

Associate professor, PhD, Digital Media Lab, Faculty of Communication, Vilnius University

Political communication, interactive networking, social media, eye tracking, publishing communication

Teresa Sylvester

Researcher, Experimental and Neurocognitive Psychology Unit, Dahlem Institute for Neuroimaging of Emotion (DINE), Center for Cognitive Neuroscience Berlin (CCNB), Free University of Berlin

Cognitive neuropsychology, reading research

Ana Vogrinčič Čepič

Assistant Professor, Department of Sociology & Department of Library and Information Science and Book Studies, Faculty of Arts, University of Ljubljana

Reading practices, sociology of reading, materiality of reading, embodied reading, reading and emotions, history of reading

Sue Walker

Professor, PhD, Department of Typography & Graphic Communication, University of Reading

Typography, materiality of text, information design